FOREX FOR BEGINNERS

A Beginners Guide to Trading Tools and Tactics

Vishnu Mohanachandran

Copyright © 2017-2018 by Vishnu Mohanachandran. All Right Reserved.
This book was published thanks to free support and training purpose

The main important
Understand yourself and emotion.
Forex is a game without using your emotions.

Forex is a game if you enter only one way to end
Lose/win
This book gives an exact idea why people lose trade
If you are one of them. Then follow all rules before you trade.
One day you will success on each trade.

......................Let's begin....................

About author

My knowledge of currency trading extends over a 5 years period and has evolved from the new binary option trading system and main reputed brokers I have developed solved and shared many trading systems for free, and I have also assisted many new traders through my various social medias forum participation.
This book for those of you who are just starting to consider trading forex or binary option but are not sure where to start this book given the abundance of information on the internet and I have deliberately kept the explanations quite simple and straight forward.

All rules you must follow, before each step. Make sure that is that doing correct directions.

End of this book each chapter have description note that you much write and clear your correction. Make sure that your idea is correct. If anyone have subjection let me know my email address I given this book.

Wish you all the best and good luck see u on trade.

TABLE OF CONTENTS

ABOUT AUTHOR	3
Table of Contents	4
CHAPTER 1.	6
SUCCESS AND FAILURE	6
A brief history of the Forex market	23
BASIC PICTURES OF TRADING TOOLS	24
MOST COMMON BEST TRADE IN HISTORY	25
What is Forex Trading	26
Individuals	27
CHAPTER 2	29
THE 10 BEST FOREX STRATEGIES	29
❖ #1: The Bladerunner Trade	29
❖ #2: Daily Fibonacci Pivot Trade	29
❖ #3: Bolly Band Bounce Trade	30
❖ #4: Forex Dual Stochastic Trade	30
❖ #5: Forex Overlapping Fibonacci Trade	30
❖ #6: London Hammer Trade	30
❖ #7: The Blade Runner Reversal	30
❖ #8: The Pop 'n' Stop Trade	31
❖ #9: The Drop 'n' Stop Trade	31
❖ #10: Trading The Forex Fractal	31
Avoid unwanted decisions	36
CHAPTER 3	45
WHAT IS MARTINGALE STRATEGY	45
What is the Martingale Strategy	56
Martingale in binary option	57

Examples: -	60
DISCERPTION NOTE	**64**
CHAPTER 4	**66**
WHY MARTINGALE IS NOT A GOOD IDEA FOR BINARY OPTIONS	**66**
Volume Based Binary Option Trading	71
DISCERPTION NOTE	**74**
CHAPTER 5	**76**
SECRET OF MARTINGALE STRATEGY	**76**
CHAPTER 6	**84**
INDICATORS MAINLY USING IN MARTINGALE STRATEGY	**84**
CHAPTER 7	**86**
CANDLESTICKS / CANDLESTICK PATTERNS	**86**
THE NERDY TRADER WHO MADE MILLIONS BY USING COMPUTER TRADING PROGRAMS	100
HE WAS ONCE A TAXI CAB DRIVER BUT NOW HE'S WORTH $5 BILLION	101
DISCERPTION NOTE	**108**
TRADE NOTE	**111**
A BRIEF HISTORY OF FOREX	**122**

CHAPTER 1.

SUCCESS AND FAILURE

What is it about successful Forex traders that sets them apart from the rest? A well-known figure in the Forex world is that 95% of Forex traders fail. While no real proof of this number exists, I can vouch for the fact that it's very close to 100%. So, what is it that puts these traders in the top 5 percent?

SUCCESSFUL FOREX TRADERS THINK DIFFERENTLY

We've all heard the typical reasons such as experience, discipline and fortitude. But what is it that really makes them tick? In this article I'm going to break down nine of the lesser-known characteristics that successful Forex traders have in common.

By successful I mean consistently profitable, first and foremost. But I would argue that success in anything is also measured by level of happiness and overall quality of life. Therefore, we'll define a successful Forex trader as someone who's trading for the right reasons and is able to achieve his or her goals through trading the Forex market.

Before we begin, I'd like to make one thing crystal clear. There's a lot of talk out there (and has been for some time) about whether anyone can consistently profit from trading Forex.

I know because I used to be the person who would search for proof on the internet. I was searching for some ray of hope that might help justify the endless torture I was putting myself through in those first three years of my trading career.

Here's my take on it… I'm certainly part of "anyone" so the answer is a resounding "yes", anyone can consistently profit trading Forex. Don't ever let someone tell you differently. You're the only one who can determine whether you become profitable. You're in control – you always have been and always will be.

So, what's the secret to success? Sorry to say, the only secret is that there is no secret. While there's no true secret to success, there is a bit of advice that will absolutely determine whether you become profitable. It's something that every single successful Forex trader has in common, and it's non-negotiable.

Never give up!

The problem is that, so many Forex traders struggle for years, and then just before their breakthrough moment they throw in the towel. Or they take a two-year hiatus and are forced to start all over again.

I know because I hear the stories. The ones about how James William tried for two years to make this Forex thing work, but he just wasn't cut out for it. What Joe failed to realize is that his "ah ha" moment was just around the corner.

This applies to all ventures in life, but it's never been truer than it is when it comes to becoming a successful Forex trader. Now that that's cleared up, let's look at some other key characteristics that successful Forex traders have in common. This is by no means a complete list, but it does cover some of the more important (and less common) characteristics.

THEY DON'T "LOSE

Before the emails start pouring in, let me explain…
No Forex trader is without losses. But there's a distinct difference between how the beginning trader loses and how the successful Forex trader loses. What is it?
To put it succinctly – mindset.
Most starting out in the Forex market view a loss as a bad thing. It's a way of signaling that they did something wrong. And doing something wrong is bad. At least that's what we've come to believe over the course of our lives.
But the successful trader doesn't view it as a "bad" thing. It's not a punishment because the Forex market isn't able to punish. It doesn't know where you entered the market or where your stop loss was, so how could it possibly punish you?
It can't.
Don't get me wrong, nobody likes to see a trade go against them. I don't care if you've been trading for one month or ten years, making money is much more enjoyable than losing money. But just because a trade doesn't go your way doesn't mean you should take it personally. Thinking this way will only dig the hole deeper.
The successful Forex trader has the mindset that a loss is simply feedback.

It's the market's way of disproving a trade setup. That's the only thing the Forex market can do, because it doesn't know anything about you or where you entered the market, nor does it care.

Losses can be a powerful way to learn. But just remember that even a trade that ends up as a loss can be the right decision. How is that possible? If you've defined your edge, and the setup met all your criteria to enter the market, then you did all you can do. The rest is up to the market, and some days the market just doesn't play along.
he average forex trader loses money, which is a very discouraging fact. But why? Put simply, human psychology makes trading difficult.

We looked at over 43 million real trades placed on some major FX broker's trading servers from Q2, 2014 – Q1, 2015 and came to some very interesting conclusions. The first is encouraging: traders make money most of the time as over 50% of trades are closed out at a gain.

Average Profit/Loss per Winning and Losing Trades per Currency Pair

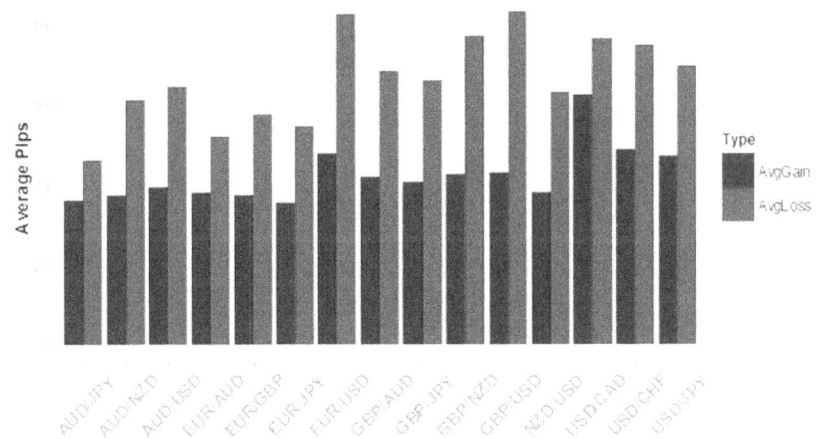

Next time you have a loss, analyze it as constructive feedback to see how you could improve the next time. Just keep in mind that even an A+ setup doesn't always work out.

I've had many trade setups that didn't work out that I would gladly take every single week. That's because I know that my edge will win out over time and put money in my account. In fact, a good exercise after a losing trade is to ask yourself, "would I take this same setup again next week if it presented itself?" You should always be able to answer this question with a resounding "yes". If you answer with a "no", you need to take a step back, figure out where it went wrong and correct it for the next trade.

A far too common saying is that trading losses are the cost of doing business. While I agree that they're inevitable, I don't agree with the analogy. Instead of labeling a loss as a business cost, why not think of it as a business investment? Each loss is an investment in your trading business and ultimately your trading education. This is a much more constructive way of spending your money.

The money you put at risk on any given trade, whether it's $5 or $500, is an investment with the best Forex coach in the world – the market. Keep an open mind and it'll show you everything you need to know.

THEY USE PRICE ACTION

Every successful Forex trader I've ever met uses price action in some way, shape or form. This doesn't mean they're using price action in the same way I use it, but they are using some form of price action as part of their trading strategy.

Whether a trader is using raw price action or simply to identify key levels in the market, price action plays a major role in any strategy. That's because it serves as a representation of the psychology within a market. It gives us some insight into the minds of other traders.

Having some idea of where buy and sell orders are in the market is critical to becoming a successful Forex trader. It can strengthen any trading strategy by providing areas to watch for potential entries as well as profit targets.

Trading Forex without using some form of price action is like trying to drive a car with one eye closed. It can be done, but I wouldn't recommend it.

THEY HAVE A DEFINED EDGE

I see a lot of talk around the internet about the need for a trader to develop an edge and define it. And if I'm honest, most of what I've read out there is pretty alarming. It's little wonder why so many traders have trouble understanding the importance. So, what exactly is an "edge" and why is it important?

An edge (in my book) is everything about the way you trade that can help put the odds in your favour. It's a combination of the time frame you trade, the price action strategies you use, the key levels you've identified, your risk to reward ratio, etc

It even goes as far as your pre-and post-trade routine. How do you handle losses? What do you do when you win? These are all things that make up your trading edge.

Although there are dozens of factors that make up your edge, you don't have to master all of them at once. Nor do you have to master all of them to start putting the odds in your favour. It's perfectly natural to master one set of factors and then slowly expand to others to further define your edge. Not only is this natural, it's the preferred way to learn.

Have you ever heard the saying, "jack of all trades, master of none"? If you try to master too many of these factors at once, you're setting yourself up to become good at a lot of factors that make up your edge.

Instead, become a master of two or three factors. You'll find this to be the fast track to becoming profitable, and much less stressful than trying to become good at twenty factors. Once you've mastered those three or four things, expand to others to continue stacking the odds in your favour.

For example, master identifying key levels along with a price action strategy such as the pin bar. This is really all you need to start seeing your profit curve rise. Then once you're comfortable with those two, strengthen your trading edge by learning stop loss strategies or different entry and exit strategies.

The key is to only tackle one or two factors at a time. Using a slow and steady approach will get you on the road to becoming a successful Forex trader in no time.

THEY AREN'T TRYING TOO HARD

But trying hard is what it takes, right? …

Wrong.

This might apply to other ventures in life, but Forex is the exception. Successful Forex traders know that trying too hard is a sign that something isn't right.

This is different from studying hard. As a new trader to Forex, studying the market to include how different currency pairs move is highly recommended. But trying to make a trading strategy work will only lead to destructive behaviour, such as emotional trading.

Jack Schwager, Author of the Market Wizards series said it best when he said, "good trading should be effortless". I'm a big fan of this book series. You can find these books here if you're interested in a good read.

I remember when I first started trading Forex, I would spend countless hours studying setups over the weekend; and not just in one sitting. I would often come back to my trading desk multiple times on Saturday and Sunday. Then on Monday, often I would end up taking a completely different trade setup only to watch the original setup move in the intended direction without me.

Sound familiar? I was trying too hard to make it work…

As soon as I stopped over-analysing trade setups and trying to make them work, my profit curve started to rise. Now I spend maybe 20 minutes per day looking at my charts. The exception being the charts I post on this site of course.

As counter-intuitive as it may seem, learning to not try as hard was one of the things that completely changed my trading career for the better. Learn to trust your intuition and stop second guessing yourself.

Successful Forex traders have taken note of this, which is why they let the market do the heavy lifting for them.

THEY THINK IN TERMS OF MONEY RISKED

It's often the smallest things in life that effect the greatest improvement. The concept of thinking in terms of money risked as it applies to Forex trading is no exception. It's an extremely simple concept that can have a huge impact on your journey to becoming a successful trader.

I've never met a successful Forex trader who didn't know how much money they were risking on any given trade. You may think that's an obvious statement, but a surprising number of traders don't think about how much money is at risk before opening a trade. This is because they're using an arbitrary percentage to calculate risk, such as one or two percentage of their trading account balance.

Think about your last trade for a moment. Did you define the exact dollar amount at risk before putting on the trade? Or were you more focused on the number of pips and the percentage of your account at risk?

The convenience of Forex position size calculators has made it so that we never have to consider the amount of money at risk. This convenience has caused a huge oversite.

Don't get me wrong, I use the position size calculator at the link above before each and every trade. However, I'm only interested in how much money is at risk – I could care less about the percentage (within reason of course).

Isn't it the same thing? Yes and no.

Obviously 2% of $5,000 is $100. In that respect the 2% and the $100 are essentially the same thing. However, in terms of the way our mind perceives these two figures they're at opposite ends of the spectrum.

I wrote an article a while back called, Pips and Percentages Will Only Get You So Far. In it I talk about the need to think in terms of money risked vs. pips or percentages. This is because pips and percentages carry no emotional value. So, when you define your risk on a trade as a percentage, it only triggers the logical side of your brain and leaves the emotional side searching for more.

This means that when you think in terms of a percentage, you're only defining your risk, but you aren't accepting it. As soon as you convert that percentage to a dollar amount, your mind is able to visualize what $100 looks like. This enables you to determine if you're prepared to lose that $100. In other words, is the trade setup in question good enough for your $100?

It's much easier to risk 2% without fully accepting the potential loss because it doesn't carry the emotional value that money does.

Successful Forex traders know this. That's why they always define their risk in terms of money. They may use a percentage as a threshold of how much they're allowed to risk, but when it comes to fully accepting the risk before putting on the trade, money is the only way to think.

THEY DON'T NEED THE MONEY

There aren't many guarantees in the Forex market. But one guarantee I can make without a shadow of a doubt is that there's no successful Forex trader who is trading today for money he needs tomorrow. In other words, trading Forex to gain a certain amount of money within a specific period.

I'm not saying that you can't generate most of your income from trading Forex and do it full time. I would be contradicting myself if I made that statement.

What I am saying is that no successful Forex trader needs a win today to pay the electric bill tomorrow. No trader can sustain that kind of pressure and become consistently profitable. That kind of environment will only foster destructive emotions like fear and greed.

This topic takes us back to the fact that successful Forex traders don't try too hard. If you need the money from trading to pay bills, odds are that you'll feel pressured to win. If you're feeling pressured to win you'll most certainly be trying too hard instead of allowing the market to do the heavy lifting.

You should only trade with money you're prepared to lose. Don't trade with the money you need to pay rent.

Likewise, don't allow the money to be your sole reason for trading. Of course, the desire for money is what attracted us to trading in the first place, but don't let it become your only desire.

Embrace the challenge and focus on the journey to becoming a successful Forex trader and the money will come.

Instead of seeing a loss as a reason to hop back in the market, take it as a signal to look at what you could have done differently. Remember, it's just feedback.

THEY KNOW WHEN TO WALK AWAY

Of course, I'm talking about taking a breather, not walking away altogether. All successful Forex traders know when to walk away and take a break. Those who are truly passionate about trading Forex know how hard it can be sometimes to walk away from the market. But it's necessary to become a successful trader.

Walking away can be especially difficult after a trade. This is because our emotions are running wild and often get the best of us. But that's exactly why walking away now can be beneficial.

After a Win

After a win we're feeling good about ourselves and our trading strategy. It feels like things are finally starting to click. Walking away now can feel like walking away from the TV after your favorited sports team just scored. But walking away now. might be exactly what you need.

Taking a break after a win will allow your emotions to settle. After the win you're feeling excited and proud of yourself, and you have every right to be. But pride and excitement have no place in the Forex market.

So, the next time you have a winning trade, pat yourself on the back and then walk away. By the time you come back to your trading desk your emotions will be under control and you'll be ready to approach the market in a neutral state of mind.

After a Loss

What do you do immediately following a loss? I can't speak for you, but I know what I used to do. I would immediately start going through all my charts looking for a new setup. This is a trap!

If you're doing this, it means your emotions are getting the best of you. After a loss it's far too easy to feel as though you need to win your money back.

So why is the failure rate so high for Forex traders?

Simply put, most traders haven't yet learned how to lose. Our emotions will always try to outweigh our logic after a loss; it's human nature. The key to becoming successful isn't about eliminating emotions after a loss, it's about channelling them in a way that will make you a better trader.

The successful Forex trader knows this, and has learned how to control these emotions. Often the process of controlling these emotions begins with walking away to take a break.

From Experience

One thing I've found helpful after a trade is to close my trading platform until the day closes at 5 pm New York time. This is when I do the bulk of my analysis anyway since I trade the daily time frame. So, it just makes sense to take a breather until then. You can of course adapt this to whatever time frame you trade.

It's a simple, yet extremely helpful way of controlling your emotions. Although it's simple, you'll likely find walking away after a trade to be one of the hardest changes you've had to make to the way you trade. But trust me when I tell you that it can have a drastic effect on your consistency and put you one step closer to becoming a successful Forex trader.

THEY DON'T FOCUS ON WINS AND LOSSES

You can't visit a Forex site these days without seeing an advertisement for some strategy that promises a 98%-win rate. Why is that? Is it because a high win rate is needed to become a successful Forex trader? Not even close!

They do it because it sells. As human beings we love to win, there's no denying it. If you've ever played sports or watched your favorited sports team on TV, I'm sure you can relate. The feeling when your favorited team wins is intoxicating.

Those behind the "strategy" that produces a supposed 98%-win rate know this and exploit it to make money.

Nobody is going to be enticed to spend money when they see a headline that promises a 50%-win rate. But what if it's a strategy with a proper risk to reward ratio that aims for $300 for every $100 risked? At a 50%-win rate that's a 20% gain on a $5,000 account over the course of 10 trades.

Successful Forex traders know this. They realized long ago that it's not about winning a high percentage of the time.

It's about maximizing the amount of money made on wins and minimizing the amount of money lost on losers.

That's not to say that all successful Forex traders use this exact risk to reward ratio. Every trader uses what works best for them. But every successful trader knows that proper risk management is critical to building a trading account, while a high win rate is usually only good for building an ego.

THEY DIDN'T GIVE UP

Although this one is last on the list, it's the most important to your success as a trader. I've found over the years that many people, including Forex traders lose sight of this very simple fact. The only way you can fail at becoming a successful Forex trader is if you give up.

This sounds obvious, but it still amazes me how often I see this trait (if you want to call it that) left out of the list of reasons why a certain trader became successful.

Here's a great example of one trader who never gave up and is now reaping the benefits…

I once met a Forex trader who had been trading for almost 30 years. This guy was trading the market before the internet was even publicly available. Back when you had to call in orders by telephone.

At any rate, as of 2011 the guy was trading an account size to where a profitable trade ranged between $50k and $100k. He has been doing something right over the past 30 years.

Someone asked him what he would attribute as the #1 reason for his success. Expecting him to say proper risk management or cutting losses, he answered with four short words…

"I never gave up"

That was his only answer to the question. He later went on to say that he had been beat down more than anyone could ever believe. Even to the point where he had lost ALL his money. Not just trading money, but every penny to his name. He was so obsessed with becoming successful that he had risked all the money he had, and lost.

Not only did he fight through it, but he went on to become a multi-millionaire. Those mistakes in his early days of trading didn't keep him down, they empowered him and fuelled his desire to become a successful Forex trader.

Cross my heart that's a true story. This guy was a retail trader using his own money, not a prop trader (although he did have a stint as a prop trader during his trading career). However, he made his millions as a retail trader.

I'm not going to mention a name (so please don't ask) because last I heard he was retiring and wanted out of the spotlight so to speak.

Just be sure to remember this story every time you get down on yourself. The next time you lose a trade or even blow up a trading account, just remember that not giving up is the #1 key to becoming a successful Forex trader.

You will never know failure if you don't give up, just as you will never taste victory if you don't persevere.

In Closing…

I hope this article has shed some light on the lesser-known characteristics of successful Forex traders. If you only remember one thing from this article, just remember to never give up and always remain patient. Becoming a successful Forex trader is a marathon, not a sprint.

Tools and techniques

Forex Analysis

Traders use Forex analysis to determine whether to buy or sell a currency pair at a given time. Forex analysis could be technical in nature, using charting tools, or fundamental in nature, using economic indicators and news based events.

Technical analysis

Technical Analysis is used to "predict" the future financial price movements based on an analysis of past price movements. Technical analysis can help investors anticipate what is "likely" to happen to prices over time. Technical analysis uses a wide variety of charts that show price over time.

Fundamental Analysis

Fundamental analysis is the examination of the underlying forces that affect the stability of the economy and companies. As with the technical analysis, the goal is to forecast future price movements, which may eventually lead to making a profit.

At the company level, fundamental analysis usually involves analyzing financial data, management, business concept and competition.

Usually, however there is also an examination of supply and demand forces for the products offered. For the national economy, fundamental analysis focuses on economic data to assess the present and future growth of the economy.

To forecast future stock prices, fundamental analysis combines economic, industry, and company analysis and derives a stock's current fair value to forecast future value

Relative Strength Index (RSI):

The RSI measures the ratio of up-moves to down-moves and normalizes the calculation so that the index is expressed in a range of 0-100. If the RSI is 70 or greater, then the instrument is assumed to be overbought (a situation in which prices have risen more than market expectations). An RSI of 30 or less is taken as a signal that the instrument may be oversold (a situation in which prices have fallen more than the market expectations).

Stochastic oscillator:

This technical tool is used to indicate overbought/oversold conditions on a scale of 0-100%. The indicator is based on the observation that in a strong up trend, period closing prices tend to concentrate in the higher part of the period's range. Conversely, as prices fall in a strong down trend, closing prices tend to be near to the extreme low of the period range. Stochastic calculations produce two lines, %K and %D that are used to indicate overbought/oversold areas of a chart. Divergence between the stochastic lines and the price action of the underlying instrument gives a powerful trading signal.

Moving Average Convergence Divergence (MACD):

This indicator involves plotting two momentum lines. The MACD line is the difference between two exponential moving averages and the signal or trigger line, which is an exponential moving average of the difference. If the MACD and trigger lines cross, then this is taken as a signal that a change in the trend is likely.

Number theory:

Fibonacci numbers: The Fibonacci number sequence (1,1,2,3,5,8,13,21,34…) is constructed by adding the first two numbers to arrive at the third. The ratio of any number to the next larger number is 62%, which is a popular Fibonacci retracement number. The inverse of 62%, which is 38%, is also used as a Fibonacci retracement number.

Gann numbers:

W.D. Gann was a stock and a commodity trader working in the '50s who reputedly made over $50 million in the markets. He made his fortune using methods that he developed for trading instruments based on relationships between price movement and time, known as time/price equivalents. There is no easy explanation for Gann's methods, but he used angles in charts to determine support and resistance areas and predict the times of future trend changes. He also used lines in charts to predict support and resistance areas.

Waves

Elliott wave theory: The Elliott wave theory is an approach to market analysis that is based on repetitive wave patterns and the Fibonacci number sequence. An ideal Elliott wave patterns shows a five-wave advance followed by a three-wave decline.

Gaps

Gaps are spaces left on the bar chart where no trading has taken place. An up gap is formed when the lowest price on a trading day is higher than the highest high of the previous day. A down gap is formed when the highest price of the day is lower than the lowest price of the prior day. An up gap is usually a sign of market strength, while a down gap is a sign of market weakness. A breakaway gap is a price gap that forms on the completion of an important price pattern. It usually signals the beginning of an important price move. A runaway gap is a price gap that usually occurs around the mid-point of an important market trend. For that reason, it is also called a measuring gap. An exhaustion gap is a price gap that occurs at the end of an important trend and signals that the trend is ending.

Trends

A trend refers to the direction of prices. Rising peaks and troughs constitute an uptrend; falling peaks and troughs constitute a downtrend that determines the steepness of the current trend. The breaking of a trend line usually signals a trend reversal. Horizontal peaks and troughs characterize a trading range.

Moving averages are used to smooth price information to confirm trends and support and resistance levels. They are also useful in deciding on a trading strategy, particularly in futures trading or a market with a strong up or down trend.

The most common technical analysis tools:

Cop pock Curve is an investment tool used in technical analysis for predicting bear market lows.

DMI (Directional Movement Indicator) is a popular technical indicator used to determine whether a currency pair is trending.

Unlike the fundamental analyst, the technical analyst is not much concerned with any of the "bigger picture" factors affecting the market, but concentrates on the activity of that instrument's market.

WHY SHOULD YOU READ THIS BOOK?

Before I'll describe forex market I'd like to say why I have choose this subject for this article. First of all, I really think that still exist people which don't know about this activity and I strongly believe that in our days it's a must, especially for those people how want to double or triple their profits from their own business. This article was created from a collection of structured data and I wish that through this article to familiarize yourself, more with the currency market.

This book all about full of my experience and research this will guide until your success every chapter I given a description from that you have write and with your understanding aspect and need to create a new strategy martingale formula

Personally, like many others I was also mistaken that it is a business only for banks. I was surprised when a friend of mine told me that this business is not only for banks and companies. He was into this business and told me that is earning good money. Later when logged on to my computer and searched for forex I was nearly shocked to see that 30% of forex industry was held by the individuals. 30% of $7 million industry means a big amount. I further searched about this forex market and got to know that it is online business now. It means anyone can be a forex trader while sitting at home in front of computer. Apparently, forex market doesn't have any common points with what we study in school but to a closer look I can say that in forex market we can find informatically, economic, marketing, mathematical, psychological and even geographical elements

WHAT IS FOREX? TRADING INTRODUCTION
WHAT IS THE FOREX MARKET?

Basically, the Forex market is where banks, businesses, governments, investors and traders come to exchange and speculate on currencies. The Forex market is also referred to as the 'Fx market', 'Currency market', 'Foreign exchange currency market' or 'Foreign currency market', and it is the largest and most liquid market in the world with an average daily turnover of $3.98 trillion.

The Fx market is open 24 hours a day, 5 days a week with the most important world trading centers being in London, New York, Tokyo, Zurich, Frankfurt, Hong Kong, Singapore, Paris, and Sydney.

It should be noted that there is no central marketplace for the Forex market; trading is instead said to be conducted 'over the counter'; it's not like stocks where there is a central marketplace with all orders processed like the NYSE. Forex is a product quoted by all the major banks, and not all banks will have the exact same price. Now, the broker platforms take all these feeds from the different banks and the quotes we see from our broker are an approximate average of them. It's the broker who is effectively transacting the trade and taking the other side of it…they 'make the market' for you. When you buy a currency pair…your broker is selling it to you, not 'another trader'

A BRIEF HISTORY OF THE FOREX MARKET:

Ok, I admit, this part is going to be a little bit boring, but it's important to have some basic background knowledge of the history of the Forex market so that you know a little bit about why it exists and how it got here. So here is the history of the Forex market in a nutshell: In 1876, something called the gold exchange standard was implemented. Basically it said that all paper currency had to be backed by solid gold; the idea here was to stabilize world currencies by pegging them to the price of gold. It was a good idea in theory, but in reality it created boom-bust patterns which ultimately led to the demise of the gold standard.

The gold standard was dropped around the beginning of World War 2 as major European countries did not have enough gold to support all the currency they were printing to pay for large military projects. Although the gold standard was ultimately dropped, the precious metal never lost its spot as the ultimate form of monetary value.

U.S. dollar being the primary reserve currency and that it would be the only currency backed by gold, this is known as the 'Bretton Woods System' and it happened in 1944 (I know you super excited to know that). In 1971 the U.S. declared that it would no longer exchange gold for U.S. dollars that were held in foreign reserves, this marked the end of the Bretton Woods System. It was this break down of the Bretton Woods System that ultimately led to the mostly global acceptance of floating foreign exchange rates in 1976. This was effectively the "birth" of the current foreign currency exchange market, although it did not become widely electronically traded until about the mid-1990s.

BASIC PICTURES OF TRADING TOOLS

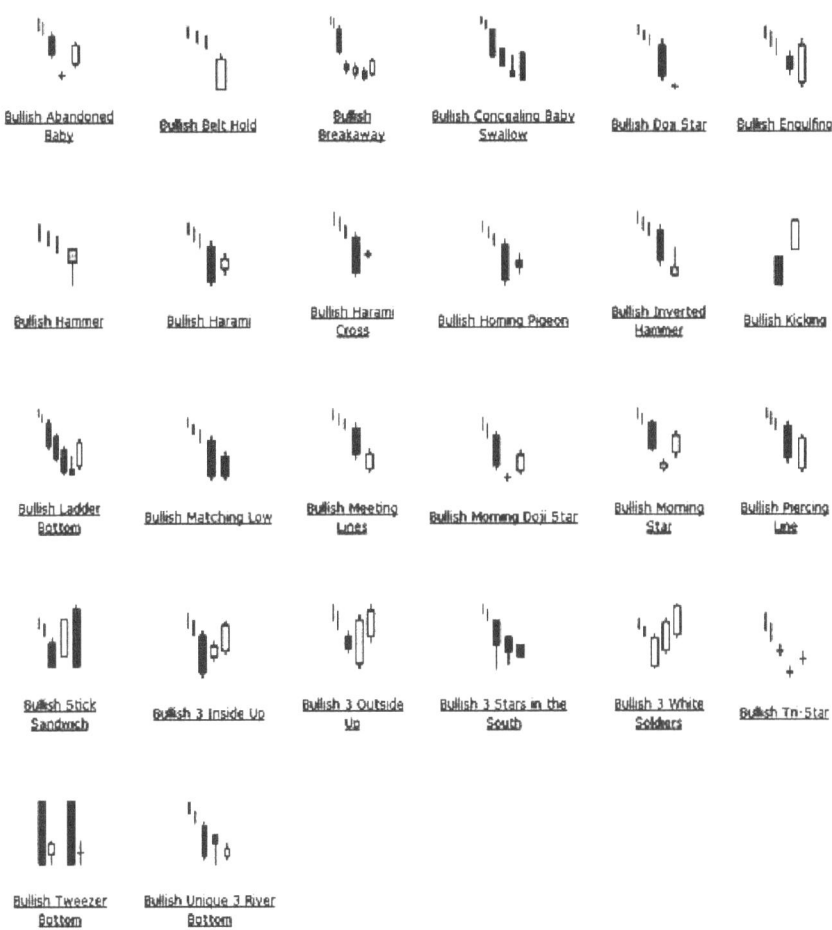

This are the main candle you may know before you trade.

MOST COMMON BEST TRADE IN HISTORY

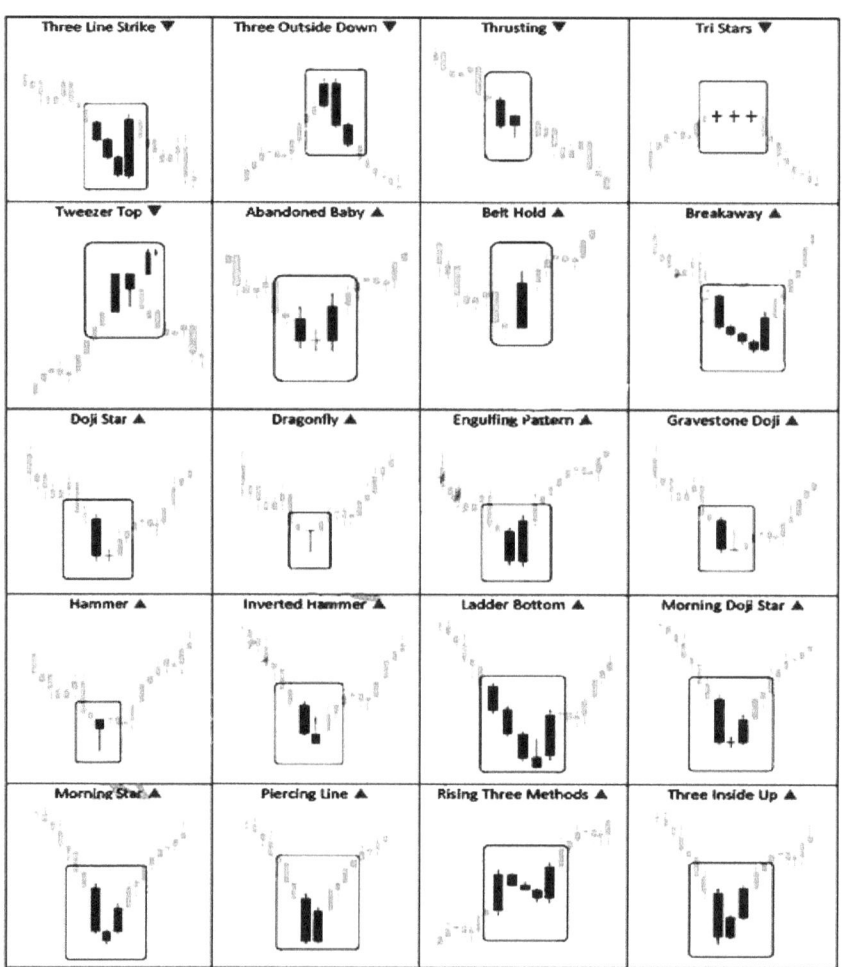

Just close look at all candle. All candle has specific story to tell mean exact place to trade. This all give you 80% profit ratio.

WHAT IS FOREX TRADING?

Forex trading as it relates to retail traders (like you and I) is the speculation on the price of one currency against another. For example, if you think the euro is going to rise against the U.S. dollar, you can buy the EURUSD currency pair low and then (hopefully) sell it at a higher price to make a profit. Of course, if you buy the euro against the dollar (EURUSD), and the U.S. dollar strengthens, you will then be in a losing position. So, it's important to be aware of the risk involved in trading Forex, and not only the reward.

Who trades Forex and why?

Companies need to use the foreign exchange market to pay for goods and services from foreign countries and to sell goods or services in foreign countries. An important part of the daily Forex market activity comes from companies looking to exchange currency to transact in other countries.

GOVERNMENTS -

A country's central bank can play an important role in the foreign exchange markets. They can cause an increase or decrease in the value of their nation's currency by trying to control money supply, inflation, and (or) interest rates. They can use their substantial foreign exchange reserves to try and stabilize the market.

HEDGE FUNDS –

Somewhere around 70 to 90% of all foreign exchange transactions are speculative in nature. This means, the person or institutions that bought or sold the currency has no plan of taking delivery of the currency; instead, the transaction was executed with sole intention of speculating on the price movement of that currency. Retail speculators (you and I) are small cheese compared to the big hedge funds that control and speculate with billions of dollars of equity each day in the currency markets.

INDIVIDUALS –

If you have ever traveled to a different country and exchanged your money into a different currency at the airport or bank, you have already participated in the foreign currency exchange market

INVESTORS –

Investment firms who manage large portfolios for their clients use the Fx market to facilitate transactions in foreign securities. For example, an investment manager controlling an international equity portfolio needs to use the Forex market to purchase and sell several currency pairs to pay for foreign securities they want to purchase

RETAILS FOREX TRADERS –

Finally, we come to retail Forex traders (you and I). The retail Forex trading industry is growing everyday with the advent of Forex trading platforms and their ease of accessibility on the internet. Retail Forex traders access the market indirectly either through a broker or a bank. There are two main types of retail Forex brokers that provide us with the ability to speculate on the currency market: brokers and dealers. Brokers work as an agent for the trader by trying to find the best price in the market and executing on behalf of the customer. For this, they charge a commission on top of the price obtained in the market. Dealers are also called market makers because they 'make the market' for the trader and act as the counter-party to their transactions, they quote a price they are willing to deal at and are compensated through the spread, which is the difference between the buy and sell price

THE MAJOR FOREX PAIRS AND THEIR NICKNAMES:

USD = US Dollar	EUR/USD = "Euro"
EUR = Euro	USD/JPY = "Dollar Yen"
JPY = Japanese Yen	GBP/USD = "Cable" or "Sterling"
GBP = British Pound	USD/CHF = "Swissy"
CHF = Swiss Franc	USD/CAD = "Dollar Canada" (CAD referred to as the "Loonie")
CAD = Canadian Dollar	
AUD = Australian Dollar	AUD/USD = "Aussie Dollar"
NZD = New Zealand Dollar	NZD/USD = "Kiwi"

CHAPTER 2

THE 10 BEST FOREX STRATEGIES

IMPORTANT RULES NEED TO FOLLOW

I really want to tell you the main important mistake all people do you know what is that? it's behavior. the main rules using martingale strategy need to follow this all rules.

- Control your emotions.
- Trade market when is active.
- Avoid the same directions.
- Make own comfortable currency pair.
- Avoid unwanted decisions.

The all details will mention below after the first chapters

❖ #1: The Bladerunner Trade

The Blade Runner is an exceptionally good **EMA crossover strategy**, suitable across all timeframes and currency pairs. It is a trending strategy that tries to pick breakouts from a continuation and trade the retests.

❖ #2: Daily Fibonacci Pivot Trade

Fibonacci Pivot Trades combine Fibonacci **retracements** and extensions with daily, weekly, monthly and even yearly pivots. The emphasis in the discussion here is on using these combinations with daily pivots only, but the idea can easily be **extended** to longer timeframes incorporating any combination of pivots.

❖ #3: Bolly Band Bounce Trade

The Bolly Band Bounce Trade is perfect in a **ranging market**. Many traders use it in combination with confirming signals, to great effect. If Bollinger Bands appeal to you, this one is well worth a look.

❖ #4: Forex Dual Stochastic Trade

The Dual Stochastic Trade users two stochastics – one slow and one fast – in combination to pick areas where **price is trending but overextended** in a short term retracement, and about to snap back into a continuation of the trend.

❖ #5: Forex Overlapping Fibonacci Trade

Overlapping Fibonacci trades are the favorites of some traders I have known. If used on their own, their reliability can be a little lower than some of the other strategies, but if you use them in conjunction with appropriate **confirming** signals, they can be extremely accurate.

❖ #6: London Hammer Trade

The extra volatility you get **when London opens** presents some unique opportunities. The London Hammer Trade is my take on an attempt to capitalize on these opportunities. Especially effective during the London session, it can be used at any time when price is likely to be taking off strongly in one direction, and possibly reversing from an area of support/resistance just as strongly.

❖ #7: The Blade Runner Reversal

As mentioned above, the Blade Runner is a trend following strategy. The Blade Runner reversal just as effectively picks entries from situations where the trend **reverses** and price begins to trade on the other side of the EMA's.

❖ #8: The Pop 'n' Stop Trade

If you've ever tried to chase price when it bounds away to the upside, only to suffer the inevitable loss when it just as quickly reverses, you will want the **secret** of the pop and stop trade in your trader's arsenal. There is a **simple trick** to determining whether price will continue in the direction of the breakout, and you must know it in order to profit from these situations.

❖ #9: The Drop 'n' Stop Trade

The flip side of the pop and stop, this strategy trades savage breakouts to the downside.

❖ #10: Trading The Forex Fractal

The forex fractal is not just a strategy but a concept of **market fundamentals** that you really need to know in order to understand what price is doing, why it is doing it, and who is making it move. This is the kind of inside info that took me years and many **thousands of dollars** to learn. It's yours here

for **free**, so make use of it   There are also several sites on the net offering **free strategies**. The problem with most of these sites is, as mentioned above, they just give a **brief** description of each strategy, with little real proof that they work. Consequently, there is a need for greater research on your part before using any of those strategies in your actual trading. Once you have selected a strategy from one of these sources you will of course need to thoroughly back test **and** forward test it. The various processes for this are covered in Forex Strategy Testing There are also several **commercial systems** to consider. Since these are more comprehensive than the simple strategies presented above, and thereby fall into the definition of Forex Trading System, they are dealt with separately in the following section, Forex Trading Systems.

CONTROL YOUR EMOTIONS

this is the first main important rule you must follow when we loss the first trade doesn't put you f**k emotion on your trade that can be loss you all balance in your account. some people chase the trend example

Trade	Amount		Win/loss(250usd)	
Call	7	90%	-7	243
Call	15	90%	-15	228
Put	31	90%	-31	197
Call	63	90%	-63	134
Put	127	90%	-127	7
When is the market is down all your trade like that the				

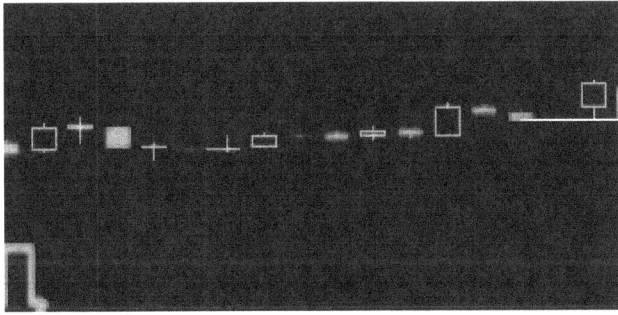

then they never follow the rules make them mind f**king shit. Most of traders they lose the trading because of keep putting random number of amount in that trade when they fail 3 times if you feel the market is slow don't mix with your emotions and trade. It is the first important lesson be a goof trader.

TRADE MARKET WHEN IS ACTIVE

Mainly all beginner trader they never look market condition just start a trade like pro if its market dead (means there is no event) try to avoid the trading on that situations can be loss.
It makes big impact on your balance.
There is some basic thing we need to check the market condition good or not the first think.
Better chart (means need check coming event happening or not)
Example - Like Trump going to invest 60 Million on federal back its that event we must utilize before we trade we know what going to happen in USD dollar that time it's give you high/low volatility on chart

AVOID THE SAME DIRECTIONS

The second main rule on martingale strategy need to avoid the same direction. Its means when u trade attitude need to remove like always click on buy option and always use sell option It's important that u didn't make it, but u must obey the martingale strategy If you break it cost you a huge of amount
Or check the trend use your mind which way the price goes use some indicator like moving average or trend line that is the better option you can win 80% trade

Without knowing the economic calendar. Don't push yourself to trade the same direction its most dangers thing you will lose money while using martingale strategy

OWN COMFORTABLE CURRENCY PAIR

Most commonly in currency market trader prefer EUR/USD. But martingale strategy you must choose which one have the high return. Unless you choose 50% profit currency pair you cannot work out on martingale strategy
This are the most currency pairs on markets
One most thing while choosing currency pair you much have the knowledge on market conations. Most of time every currency doesn't have that much event on martingale strategy event not a most important thing. The important is the currency combination and return.
The good chart is most important. Example I will give below that kind of chart id you seen while trading supposed to analyze the chart and processed and make yourself to ready for trade.

Symbol	Currency Pair	Treading Term
GBP/USD	British Pound / US Dollar	"Cable"
EUR/USD	Euro / US Dollar	"Euro"
USD/JPY	US Dollar / Japanese Yen	"Dollar Yen"
USD/CHF	US Dollar / Swiss Franc	"Swissy"
USD/CAD	US Dollar / Canadian Dollar	"Dollar Canada"
AUD/USD	Australian Dollar / US Dollar	"Aussie Dollar"
EUR/GBP	Euro / British Pound	"Euro Sterling"
EUR/JPY	Euro / Japanese Yen	"Euro Yen"
EUR/CHF	Euro / Swiss Franc	"Euro Swiss"
GBP/CHF	British Pound / Swiss Franc	"Sterling Swiss"
CHF/JPY	Swiss Franc / Japanese Yen	"Swiss Yen"
GBP/JPY	British Pound / Japanese Yen	"Sterling Yen"

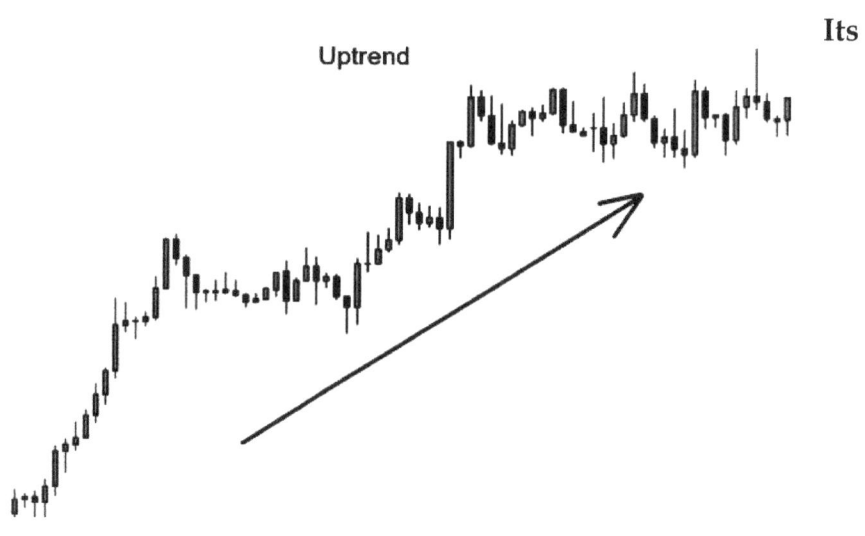

Its

perfect examples of uptrend

Its perfect examples of uptrend

This the perfect examples of down trend
In this chart you can see how it's possible to use trend line

AVOID UNWANTED DECISIONS.

This commonly I saw on people how trying to make money on faster and when they lose money they never follow the strategy they only follow mind. Examples when the trader using martingale strategy and they break between the rules

7	Lost
15	Lost
31	Lost
100	Lost

When they think...! ohhhh f***k I lost 31 USD. Let's cross the finger cover the previous loss and gain some profit then they try to put 100 USD at last loss everything. Need to keep in mind always follow the rules that main important and when you lose 5 bets don't try cover up leave it for that day and try next day with you fresh mind and start with zero

HANDS-FREE FOREX TRADING

This is basically an old post that I've brought to the top of the blog to try and spark a bit of conversation about the topic of forex robots. A few years back when I first wrote this post, automated trading was all the rage, and every man and his dog was selling forex robots that supposedly turned paupers into overnight millionaires.

We all know better by now of course, or at least those of us who researched automated trading certainly do. I worked with automated trading robots over many years. I had some success, but never quite enough to switch from manual trading entirely.

But in the last six months I've been drifting back to the topic, and the auto trading scene that I've discovered these days has really surprised me.

Firstly, there are many advanced tools available (at a price, Ouch!) that speed the process up. This can be handy when you're trying to test out all the various parameters for a strategy you've been working on. What used to take me months or years, I can now achieve much faster, sometimes in a few days.

Secondly, the market has matured with respect to auto trading. We now have a better idea of what works and what doesn't.

Finally, from my own point of view, refinement of the principles of Price Action trading has given me a very clear idea of where I want to go in the robots I design. And the fact that I will be basing these automated strategies I'm going to build on the principles of pure Price Action, should give me an edge compared to the strategies I was working with years ago, which were based on arbitrary indicators and so on.

So over the next several months I will be working on building a portfolio of automated trading strategies. Several of the 10 best forex strategies available on this site, are likely candidates. I also have one early running strategy that shows great promise, and if all goes well I will be offering it free to those who join what I am at this stage calling, The Robot Development Group. More details as the weeks go by.

In the meantime, tell me what you think. Would you be interested in a series of posts on this topic? What aspects would you like discussed? And what about the Robot Development Group, would you be interested in joining, and if so what would you like the group to involve itself in?

At this stage I have a bunch of ideas, based around the development group members interactive involvement in the robot development. There would also be things like discounts available for robots that are eventually released, and maybe free signals while they are in development. Perhaps access to a private Facebook forum as well. Everything is available for discussion now, as I'm just in the early stages of putting this together. And of course, I'd want to know whether you're prepared to pay for membership of such a group, and how much you would pay.

So, here is that old post for you to read first up. And then, most importantly, leave your questions and feedback in the comments area at the bottom of the page. If you email me questions regarding this, I will post them and answer them here, so that we all have access to everyone's input.

   Cheers,

Traders are increasingly turning to the three broad areas of hands free forex trading – using forex signals providers, automated trading software and forex managed accounts – for some or even all of their trading.

There are many reasons for this, ranging from not having enough time to concentrate on real time chart-watching trades, not having the inclination to manually trade, not trusting your ability to trade, inability to handle the stress associated with manual trades, lack of confidence due to insufficient knowledge of the markets, diversification etc.

For a trader who fits into any of the above categories, the attraction of having either an automated forex trading program or professional trader do their trading for them is obvious. And many of us who enjoy manual trading also like to have our trading efforts diversified in this manner.

I have used forex robots extensively in the past, and still do. I also devote a certain percentage of my trading account to managed accounts. My reasons for doing this are that it allows me to cover timeframes and time zones that I would otherwise not be able to trade in, and because it helps to have different approaches mixed in with my own.

Like any area of trading, the automated and semi-automated approaches need caution in their implementation. Whether you're thinking of using robots, signals or account managers, you will need to exercise due diligence. There is a very wide spread of qualities across all three approaches.

Some robots such as the Kangaroo have performed magnificently, while others such as Forex Growth Bot have proved to be a great disappointment in recent times.

The same can be said with respect to signals service providers and managed account funds. Some are good, some not so good and some downright bad.

If you'd like to take the subject further, go to the sections of the site devoted to Forex Signals, Forex Robots or Forex Managed Accounts.

AUTOMATED FOREX TRADING SOFTWARE

otherwise known as Expert Advisors or Robo can mean trading without emotion or hassles

This is the second of three methods of hands off trading that the forex trader may consider, the others being Forex Managed Accounts and Forex Signal Service.

Forex trading software doesn't have to be automated; many successful traders only ever trade manually. But I am assuming that you have an interest in automation if you are reading this section.

So, just exactly what do people mean by automated trading software? Simply put, a trading robot is a software program that executes a trading strategy automatically, with no need for ongoing input from an external source (i.e. the trader). They are also sometimes referred to as Expert Advisors or EA's.

Some years ago, I was speaking to a broker about EA's and said something like "we all know they don't work". In the next 5 min that broker managed to persuade me to take another look at forex robots.

Of course, I was thinking "hey, you're a broker, you get paid every time the software trades. And we all know they trade a lot, a nice little earner for you!"

Nonetheless, my curiosity had been roused so I went and did some research. What I discovered completely changed my mind.

Since then I've taken an active interest in the subject. While not claiming to be an expert in the technicalities, I have observed the results of auto trading systems enough to convince me that there are a handful of robots that can be trusted with your money.

I don't say put all your faith in any one forex.; of course, the usual risk management and diversification issues apply. However, I now devote a portion of my own personal trading account to forex robots

Why?

There are many reasons for adopting a hands-off approach to your forex trading. These mainly center around the following issues:

The benefits of absentee trading. Being able to walk away from your computer knowing that a piece of software is doing the job for you frees you up to live your life any way you like. As a human being, it is impossible for you to trade 24/7. Robots do this without complaint You'll never miss a trade again…

Emotional issues in trading. Automated trading software is totally unemotional. You can set it up to trade the way you would like to trade (as an ice cool trader, presumably) and entrust the job to it. The robot will do exactly as you had planned, without any of the distractions of niggling thoughts, doubts etc. entering the decision. It's a good option for dealing with the trader demons of fear and greed.

Entry cost. The market for robots is extremely competitive and this has driven the price down over time. Considering the performance of some of the better robots, the money you pay upfront can soon be recouped if you trade it on a reasonably sized account. (Disclaimer: always trial the forex in a demo account first until you are comfortable with its performance)

Research edge: you pay a small amount of money upfront for a piece of software which has been thoroughly researched and tested, with a proven performance track record. No need to spend months or years developing your own system.

Proven performance. You simply do your own research on the available offerings, and select the robot that both suits you and has a proven track record. Again, a big timesaver, if you get it right!

Automated trading software can be a great way for beginners to observe how a professional trader approaches the market. This gets back to emotional issues, the plague of all forex currency trading beginners. If you select wisely, and only place the robot on a demo account or small live account, you can sit back and "see how it should be done" at your leisure. This was one of the first things that struck me when I started using robots. I would be watching the behavior of the EA during a trade and contrasting the way it managed to trade to the way I would be tempted to manage the trade. The robot usually did a much better job than me It's like having a mentor do your trading for you while you stand behind them observing and learning.

Many vendors of forex robots offer a money back guarantee, enabling you to get a refund inside a certain trial period. This can be anything from one to three months, as a rule. This should be seen as a bonus when considering selection of an EA, not a deal breaker. It may be that one robot is excellent, but gives no money back guarantee, while another robot that is absolute rubbish cheerfully refunds your money if you're not satisfied. The reasoning is obvious: the vendor of the rubbish robot knows that a certain percentage of customers will for one reason or another (laziness, didn't know about the guarantee etc.) fail to redeem their money.

Finally, and considering all the above, you may prefer spending time with family and friends than watching charts! But what about the downsides to using automated forex trading software?

You will most likely want to have a VPS service on which to run the forex robot. This is an extra ongoing, albeit small cost. See VPS services

The very utility of having a robot trade for you without your input can be a source of constant low-level tension for some people. You may find yourself worrying "What is it doing now? God, I hope it hasn't lost me any money!" There are some people who just must CONTROL every aspect of their trading. Automated trading software is probably not a good fit for these people.

There can be a difficulty in locating a robot that trades the way you want it to, while meeting your other requirements with regards to cost etc. For example, a great many robots scalp the market, and are not suitable for someone whose vision is longer term.

The performance of forex robots generally degrades over time as market conditions change and the code for the robot is "cracked" i.e. stolen and mass distributed. It's important to monitor performance against your initial expectations, and be prepared to stop trading at the first sign that the robot is no longer doing its job. This can be temporary while you continue to run the EA in a demo account, or permanent if the software shows no recovery in its performance over time.

Last but most definitely not least, anyone thinking of using auto trading software must understand the risks involved. There is a good reason why most robots return a very high win to loss rate (often above 80%, sometimes even 90%). That reason is that simply having such a high win rate means that when you do suffer a loss, that loss is substantial. You must be able to psychologically absorb the occasional such loss in the face of a streak of much smaller wins. It is simple mathematical probability that an automated system that wins 90% of the time has wins that are much smaller than its losses

If you have lasted this far I guess you are still interested in the possibility of using forex robots. In that case, you may wish to consider the list below under the link to Automated Forex Trading Software. Please note that the usual disclaimer applies to these recommendations: Do Your Own Research and remember that past performance is no guarantee of future results:

Click the following link to go to Automated Forex Trading Software

Got an idea for something you'd like coded into a robot? Click the following link to go to Expert Advisor Coding

The second approach to automation of your trading covered is Forex Managed Accounts.

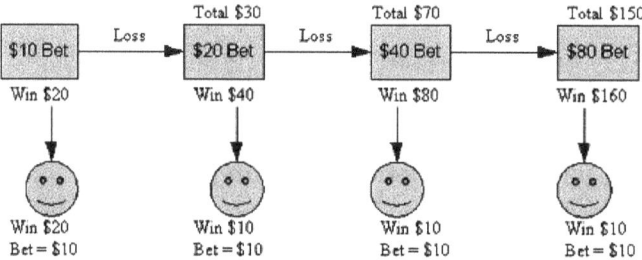

Martingale System Overview

Chapter 3

What is Martingale strategy

Would you be interested in a trading strategy that is practically 100% profitable? Most traders will probably reply with a resounding "Yes!" Amazingly, such a strategy does exist and dates all the way back to the 18th century. This strategy is based on probability theory, and if your pockets are deep enough, it has a near-100% success rate.
Known in the trading world as the martingale, this strategy was most commonly practiced in the gambling halls of Las Vegas casinos. It is the main reason why casinos now have betting minimums and maximums, and why the roulette wheel has two green markers (0 and 00) in addition to the odd or even bets. The problem with this strategy is that to achieve 100% profitability, you need to have very deep pockets; in some cases, they must be infinitely deep.
No one has infinite wealth, but with a theory that relies on mean reversion, one missed trade can bankrupt an entire account. Also, the amount risked on the trade is far greater than the potential gain. Despite these drawbacks, there are ways to improve the martingale strategy. In this article, we'll explore the ways you can improve your chances of succeeding at this very high-risk and difficult strategy.

HOW TO TRADE?

- Any currency pair and timeframe will work.
- Determine your basic position size.
- Place an order in a random direction (Buy or Sell) with some fixed stop-loss and the same take-profit.
- After the SL or TP is triggered you either win or lose.
- If you win, set the position size to the initial and go the step 3.
- If you lose, double the position size and go to step 3.
- If you have infinite trading account balance, eventually you'll win a lot. If your account balance is limited, you'll lose it eventually.

DEFINITION of '**Anti-Martingale** System' A system of position sizing that correlates the levels of investment with the risk and portfolio size. An **anti-Martingale** strategy involves halving your bets each time you lose a trade, and doubling them each time you win a trade.

This system is generally played with an even money game such as the red/black bet in roulette or the pass/don't pass bet in craps and is known as the Martingale. The idea is that by doubling your bet after a loss, you would always win enough to cover all past losses plus one unit

A submartingale is a kind of stochastic process; one in which the expected value of next period's value, as projected on the basis of the current period's information, is greater than or equal to the current period's value

A martingale is a type of dog collar that provides more control over the animal without the choking effect of a slip collar. Martingale dog collars are also known as greyhound, whippet or humane choke collars. ... The larger loop is slipped onto the dogs neck and a lead is then clipped to the smaller loop

RISKS OF A MARTINGALE STRATEGY

A Martingale forex strategy offers a risky way for traders to bet that that long-term statistics will revert to their means. Forex traders use Martingale cost-averaging strategies to average-down in losing trades. These strategies are risky and long-run benefits are non-existant.

Here's why Martingale strategies are attractive to forex traders:

First, under ideal conditions and including positive carry, Martingale strategies offer what appears to be a predictable profit outcome and a "sure bet" on eventual wins.

Second, Martingale forex strategies don't rely on any predictive ability. The gains from these strategies are based on mathematical probabilities over time, instead of relying on skillful forex traders using their own underlying knowledge and experience in particular markets. Novice traders like Martingale strategies because they can work even when the trader's "trade-picking" skills are no better than pure chance.

Third, currency pairs tend to trade in ranges over fairly long periods of time, so the same price levels are often revisited many times. As with "grid trading," there are usually multiple entry and exit possibilities in the trading range.

It's important to understand from the beginning that a Martingale forex strategy doesn't improve the chances of winning a given trade, and its major benefit is that it delays losses. The hope is that losing trades can be held until they become profitable again.

Martingale strategies are based on cost-averaging. The strategy means doubling the trade size after every loser until a single winning trade occurs. At that point, because of the mathematical power of doubling, the trader hopes to exit the position with a profit

A simple example of win-lose

The below table shows how a Martingale strategy works with a simple trading game, in which each round has a 50% chance of winning and a 50% chance of losing.

Stake	Outcome	Profit/Loss	Current Balance
$100	Won	$100	$100
$100	Won	$100	$200
$100	Lost	-$100	$100
$200	Lost	-$200	-$100
$400	Lost	-$400	-$500
$800	Won	$800	$300

In this simple example, the forex trader takes a position size worth a standard $100 in account equity. With each winning trade in that same currency pair, the subsequent position size is kept at the same $100.

If the trade is a loser, the trade size is doubled for each successive loser. This is referred to as "doubling down." If the forex trader is lucky, within a few trades he or she will enjoy a winner.

When the Martingale forex strategy wins, it wins enough to recover all previous losses including the original trade amount, plus additional gains.

In fact, a winning trade always results in a net profit. This occurs because:

$$2n = \sum 2n\text{-}1 + 1$$

Where n is the number of trades. So, the drawdown from any number of consecutive losses is recovered by the next successful trade, assuming the trader is capitalized well enough to continue doubling each trade until achieving a winner.

The main risk of Martingale strategies is the possibility that the trading account may run out of money through drawdown before a winning trade occurs.

A basic Martingale forex trading system

In real forex trading, there usually isn't a rigid binary outcome – A trade can close with a variable amount of profit or loss. Still, the Martingale strategy remains the same. The trader simply defines a certain number of pips as the profit target, and a certain number of pips as the stop-loss threshold.

In the following recent EUR/USD example showing averaging-down in a falling market, with both profit target and stop loss levels set at 20 pips.

Rate	Order	Lots	Entry	Average Entry	
Absolute drop			Break Even	Balance	
1.3500	Buy	1	1.3500	1.3500	
0.0			0.00	$0	
1.3480	Buy	2	1.3480	1.3490	-
20.0			10.00	-$2	
1.3460	Buy	4	1.3460	1.3475	-
40.0			15.00	-$6	
1.3440	Buy	8	1.3440	1.3458	-
60.0			17.50	-$14	
1.3420	Buy	16	1.3420	1.3439	-
80.0			18.75	-$30	
1.3439	Sell	16	1.3439	1.3439	-
61.2			0.00	$0	

First, the trader buys 1 lot at a price of 1.3500. The price then moves against the trader, down to 1.3480 which triggers the stop loss.

The trading system accounts 1.3480 as a "theoretical" stop loss, yet it doesn't liquidate the position. Instead, the system opens a new trade for twice the size of the existing position. So, the second line of the table above shows one more lot added to the position. This allows an average entry price of 1.3490 for the two lots.

It's important to note that the unrealized loss is the same, yet now the trader needs a retracement of only 10 pips in order to break even, not the 20 pips envisioned by a loss following the first trade.

"Averaging down" by doubling the trade size reduces the relative amount needed to recover the unrealized losses. By averaging down with even more trades, the break-even value approaches a constant level which comes ever closer to the designated stop-loss level.

Continuing the above example, at the fifth trade the average entry price is 1.3439 so when the price moves upward through that point, the overall averaged holdings reach the break-even level.

In this example, the first four trades were losses, but all were covered by the profit on the fifth trade. A mechanical forex trading system can close out this group of trades at or above the break-even level. Or, the system can hold the currency pair for greater gains.

When a Martingale strategy works successfully, the trader can recover all losses with a single winner. Still, there is always a major risk that the trader may suffer an unrecoverable drawdown while awaiting a winner.

Caveats about the Martingale forex strategy

From a mathematical and theoretical viewpoint, a Martingale forex trading strategy should work, because no long-term sequence of trades will ever lose.

Still, in the real world the perfect Martingale strategy would require unlimited capitalization, since the trader may face a very long string of losses before achieving a single winner. Few traders could withstand the required drawdown.

If there are too many consecutive losing trades, the trade sequence must be closed at a loss before starting the cycle again. Only by keeping the initial position size very small in proportion to the account equity could the trader have any chance for survival.

Ironically, the higher the total drawdown limit, the lower the probability of losing in a trade sequence, yet the bigger that loss will be if or when it occurs. This phenomenon is called a "Taleb distribution." The more trades, the more likely that a long string of losses will arise.

This issue occurs because during a sequence of losing trades with a Martingale system the risk exposure increases exponentially. In a sequence of n losing trades, the trader's exposure increases as 2n-1.

So, if the trader is forced to exit a trade sequence prematurely, the losses are very large. On the other hand, the profit from a Martingale forex trade only increases in a linear way. It is proportional to half of the average profit per trade, multiplied by the number of trades.

Regardless of the underlying trading rules used to choose currency pairs and entry points, if the trader is only right 50% of the time (the same as random chance) then the total expected gains from winning trades would be:

Profit ≈ (½ n) x G

When n is the total number of trades and G is the amount of profit on each trade.

However, a single big losing trade will reset this amount to zero. Continuing the example above, if the trader sets a limit of 10 double-down trades, the biggest trade lot size would be 1024. The maximum amount would only be lost if there were 11 losing trades in a row.

According to the above equation, the probability of this occurrence is (½)11. In other words, the trader would expect to lose the maximum amount once every 2048 trades.

After 2048 forex trades:
- Expected gains are (½) x 211 x 1 = 1024
- Expected worst single loss is -1024
- Expected net profit is 0

Assuming the trader's trade-choosing strategy is no better than simple chance, the Martingale system always offers at least a 50-50 chance of success.

Again, Martingale doesn't improve the chances of winning a trade, it simply postpones losses or helps the trader potentially avoid losses by staying in the positions long enough. It is risky, and very few traders have been successful with Martingale strategies in the long run.

Martingale forex strategies only work when currency prices are trading in a range

Some trend-following traders use a "reverse Martingale" strategy that involves doubling winning trades, and cutting losses quickly. However, Martingale strategies tend to suffer during trending markets. The only opportunities come from range-trading instead of trend-following.

The challenge is to choose currency pairs with positive carry which are range-bound instead of trending. And, the trading system should be programmed to unwind positions when steep corrections occur.

Martingale forex strategy can enhance yield

One occasional use of Martingale forex strategies is to enhance yield. Some traders use Martingale strategies with positive-carry forex trades of currency pairs with large interest-rate differentials. That way, positive credits accumulate during the open trades.

By limiting drawdown to 5% of the account equity, some traders achieve 0.5 to 0.7% monthly return by using Martingale strategies when EUR/CHF and EUR/GBP are trading in tight ranges over fairly long periods of time.

The trader must keep a watchful eye for the risks that can result when forex prices break out into new trends, especially around support and resistance levels. Again, Martingale only works with range-bound currency pairs, not trending ones.

ADVANTAGE ON MARTINGALE

As attractive as the Martingale strategy may look to both binary options traders, increasing the investment on each high-probability trading set-up, it is initially flawed by two misconceptions. The first of these is the so-called 'gamblers fallacy' and an assumption that both the roulette wheel and a financial market have a memory to remember what happened on the previous bet/trade. This assumes that since the roulette wheel has landed 15 times on red, it will realise this and throw a black in there to make amends. In fact, each roulette spin is entirely unconnected to the last and has the same probability of continuing to land on red for the eternity as far as it is concerned. Financial markets, on the other hand, do formulate memory and, whilst this is not guaranteed, the probability of a set-up is only based on history which gives a small advantage to the binary options trader using Martingale strategies to counter failed, high-probability set-ups.

The second misconception which may distinguish between using Martingale in a purely gambling sense and for trading binary options is the understanding of the chances of success. Casinos often outlive the gambler for a reason and this is that it always has a statistical 'edge' over its customers. Whilst the red and black of a roulette table may seem like a 50% game of chance, the introduction of the green '0' square makes it an unfair game over time with a skewed bias towards the success of the casino. Binary options, on the other hand, can involve methods of trading which, on extensive back-testing, can reveal a bias in favour of the trader and, therefore, the possibility that if Martingale is employed strictly can result in a favourable skew in the direction of the trader

Risk involved in Martingale strategy

The major problem for most binary options traders in using Martingale, even with a great strategy producing a 70%-win rate, is the possibility of a run of statistically improbable trades. Many binary options traders employing Martingale will have assessed, historically, that their system has only ever encountered a maximum of 6 failed trades in a row. However, since history is not a definitive predictor of future price-action, it is possible that this could be exceeded dramatically. Psychologically, and financially, a run of 9, 10 or even 11 failed trades using the multiplier of Martingale can push an account to depletion. Many strategies when seen on paper look profitable using Martingale may incur periodic drawdowns beyond the resources of the account and here lies the fundamental problem. Having said this, many binary options traders can successfully reduce the risk of this occurring by beginning by trading only a very small fraction (up to 2%) of their account. Although losses can accumulate quickly, this is the only way to mitigate the risk of an improbable, but highly possible run of account-depleting trades.

How to use martingale strategy

if the first flip of the coin is a loss of $1, on the second one he bets $2. If the gambler wins this toss he wins $4. This returns his $2 stake and he covered his loss of $1 on the first bet and on top of that he made an extra dollar. All good so far but if he loses the second toss as well, he must double up his previous bet so now he has $4 at stake. If he wins he profits $4 on the trade which will cover his previous losses and bring him an extra dollar (first loss – $1, second loss -$2, total – 3 dollars). If he loses, he will again double up the previous loss, which means he will bet $8. Ok, I'm not going to bore you anymore and just tell you that this doubling up will go on indefinitely until a win comes along. It will look like this: -$8, -$16, -$32, -$64…. hmm, long way from $1, which was our initial bet, but the point is it will cover all your previous losses and provide a $1 profit once you hit a winner. Well, in our scenario the gambler keeps trading until eventually the coin feels bad for all the losses and comes up heads for the final win. Given that our current bet was $128 (double the previous loss) we gain that amount and cover all the losses, plus $1 (all or losses summed up were -$127, basically your profits will be the current return – (the cost of the current trade + cost of the previous trade) = amount of original bet). That's about it with the explanation so let's look at the pros and cons of the strategy

WHY DOES THE MARTINGALE STRATEGY SUCK?

Think of it this way: what if the streak of losses extends to 10, which is very possible? Assuming you just started with a bet of $1, your current bet would have to be $512...and if you win that, you make a measly profit of one buck (all your previous losses are -$511). Our bets will grow exponentially with every loss and the numbers will quickly get out of control if you never win and eventually you will run out of money. This strategy has no "edge", nothing to make it work other than pure luck! It is clearly and with no doubt a gambling strategy and does nothing for you except the illusory promise of capital preservation...but maybe there is still hope for it and we could make it work in trading. Of course, before we move one, there is a bit of a problem when using martingale with binary options. For it to work as described your trades must pay 1 to 1 or 100%. If you trade $100 you have to get $200 back on a win otherwise it's a losing game. If you only get back say 80% then you only return 60% of the original trade.

DISCERPTION NOTE

This note for you decide how will you write your on-martingale strategy there are more ways to incise your betting volume the details I mention in other chapters

Chapter 4

Why Martingale is not a good idea for Binary Options

Chapter Now with digital options there are some things you must take into consideration. Number 1, you must be aware of the payout percentages because binary trading is a minus-sum game. You never win as much as you bet. Because they are less than 100% you must increase your stake with that in mind, so you cover your previous loss and gain a profit equal to the initial trade, otherwise you will end up losing no matter what happens.

For example;

If you place a trade for $100 and lose it, then make a trade for $200 and win 85% you only get back $370, covering your cost ($100 +$200) but only winning 70% of your first trade.

If you went to a third trade, a $400 trade, you would return $740 but only profit $40 or 40% of the initial trade.

If you took it to a 4th trade, only doubling the trade size, the profit shrinks again and will turn into a net loss on the 5th trade.

The real risk here is that with each trade, to ensure that you do not end up losing, you must increase you stake by more than 100%. This means that your potential losses grow exponentially with each trade. The first trade is 100%, then the second is 100% +115%, then the third is 215% + 250%, then the fourth is 465% + 500% so that your first trade is X amount of dollars, and your fourth is nearly 10X dollars and growing with each trade until your account can't handle it anymore and you are wiped out of the market. In the end, Martingale is not trading to win, its trading not to lose.

A martingale is one of many in a class of betting strategies that originated from, and were popular in, 18th century France. The simplest of these strategies, all intended for gambling and gaming, was designed for a zero-sum game, that is, a game in which each side bets the same amount and wins and losses are absolute. If I win, I win all, if you win you win all.

The basic strategy has the gambler double his bet after every loss so that the first win would recover all previous losses plus win a profit equal to the original stake. In today's world the martingale strategy is most often applied to roulette as the probability of hitting either red or black is close to 50%.

The idea behind the martingale is a simple one: Double your previous loss until you eventually win, resulting in profit no matter what, if you can go the distance. The only limiting factor is the size of your account, so long as you can make the next trade you have a 50/50 chance of making all your money back.

What Martingale really does is remove the need to understand the market, technical analysis and trading because the only thing that matters is the outcome of the next trade. All you must do be able to make a trade, and then double it if you lose.

Martingale is nearly a sure thing as your chances of producing a win grow with each consecutive trade, assuming of course you have an unlimited amount of time and a bank roll big enough to make whatever the next trade needs to be without going bankrupt. The danger lies within those assumptions.

To some, the martingale system seems pretty fail-safe, especially for newbies, but that is a popular misconception. If used incorrectly it can quickly compound one's losses to the point of catastrophic failure. The best thing to do is to use a sound money management technique like the Percent Rule to ensure that no single trade is so big it wipes you out. Save Martingale for having fun at the casino.

Money management yes/no

September 5, 2016 Posted in Articles, Learning academy, Money Management

There is already one article on our web site about martingale. You can look at it here: Martingale strategy. In this article, we will take a better and more professional look at this system from the trader's point of view.
As many of you already know, the martingale system has been created by gamblers and lies in the raising of bets (trade amounts) round after round, to achieve the increase in the number of chips on the players table.

I do not want to urge anyone to use this system. All traders are adults and have their own opinion and should be able to decide whether this system is suitable for our trading or not.

Put into terms of binary options: After every unsuccessful trade, we double the amount with which we trade. If we win – profit will be more than enough to cover previous losses. If we lose – we continue in the same spirit.
How to use martingale in binary options trade
Simple, right? But we must consider a few factors, such as profit. Roulette, where this system was developed, has a 200% payout after winning. For binary options, it is around 180%. Therefore, it will not be enough to multiply the sum by two, but by 2.3. Here is a table showing how would this system work in case of $ 10 initial trade.

Now it still looks like we took the trading of binary options not as a regular possibility of earning money, but rather as a gamble. Let me tell you something that will change this view. How to implement this strategy so that we "can't lose?"
I suppose that if you want to use a money management plan, you already have a strategy that is profitable, and you want to deal with occasional loss. Traders who have already tried a couple of trades and are somehow still at zero will certainly appreciate this system. Here are some tips on how to achieve the proper functioning of money management plan.

Basic forex strategies
Binary Options Ladder Strategy

Successfully trading in binary options requires you to be able to accurately predict the direction and extent of a given asset's price. In fact, this is essential for any kind of trading. Before you can place a trend, you must understand where the price currently is and in which direction it is moving.
You will then need to assess whether it will continue to move in that direction or whether it will change direction. On top of this you need to know how long it will be before it peaks and changes direction. These factors influence the trade you will be willing to make. Of course, you cannot get the trade right every time; you may find the direction is up for most items, but not your specific asset.
Binary options ladder trading is one solution in this type of scenario; it is rapidly growing in popularity and has proved to be a very successful approach for a variety of traders

Ladder Trading

This type of trading allows you to place several trades and cover a variety of different options. In theory you may be able to win on all the trades but if you lose on one the other two will pay out to prevent you losing out on your funds. Within binary options you will be presented with three or more price levels. Each of them will be an equal distance from the other ones; just as the rungs of a ladder are. You can then set timeframes for each price rise, breaking down a large price increase into several smaller increases and potential payouts. If the price rises as high as you expect you are likely to win on all the trades, if not then you may win on one or two; with careful calculation you can ensure that a win on one will cover the cost of all three trades. A win on two would put you into profit.

This strategy can be very useful when you are confident that a price will go upwards but there is a resistance which could affect how quickly it does this. Spitting the price rises and the trades reduces your risk.

To place a ladder trade, you will need to choose a progressive series which offers strike prices. You can then set your strike prices and a timeframe for each rise in price. The percentage provided by your broker should be very similar to what you would get if you traded the entire price rise in one go.

To fully understand this technique, it is beneficial to see an example:

Pick a currency such as USD/EUR. The current price, at 10am is 118.50. You believe that the price will rise to 125.50 before the end of the day but you are aware that there are a lot of factors which can affect it.

You then decide that the price will rise to 119.75 by 11am, to 121.50 by 1pm and 125.50 by 3pm.

The percentage payout is agreed between you and your broker. In effect you are placing three separate trades, but they are linked and dependent upon each other.
It is important to note that the rewards may be small if the price rises are small and the time frame is also small. Your broker needs to balance the risks to themselves and will offer a corresponding rate. With a little practice this can be a very successful approach to binary option trading

Look the chart and decide the moving average on this chart where you make call and where you can make put

Volume Based Binary Option Trading

One off the most important decisions a binary options trader must make is whether to place a bull or a bear put. Understanding this is an essential part of making the right decision and placing a successful trade. One approach, which will provide an excellent guide as to what most people involved with the market expect to happen, is to look at the volume of a specific asset. This is not the volume of the asset in total; it is the quantity of an asset which is being moved between people. An asset which has one hundred units and ten of them are being traded does not suggest a market which expects something to happen to the value of the asset. However, in contrast if ninety or the entire one hundred units are being moved then there is something worth looking at.

It is important to remember that the volume of an asset is across the entire market, not just the amount being traded by your binary options broker.

If you believe you have located an asset which is being traded in volume across the market, then you may want to join in and make your own trade. The first step is to locate an hourly chart which shows your specific asset. You will then be able to see the candles on the chart, showing the highs and lows of the asset. The last candle for a bear and bull market should be looked at more closely. You will need to calculate the average for the peaks and the troughs of the asset. Once you have completed this draw a horizontal line through the lows of your candle and the highs of your candle.

You will then have created your boundaries; most assets will not move outside of these lines. If the asset you are looking at is very close to one of the boundary lines you should consider placing a trade which is the opposite of the current trend. Alternatively, if it currently near the middle but moving in one direction you could place a trade with the asset movement.

Volume is an important technique to confirm the way you are reading the chart and your gut instinct. If there is a large amount of movement on the market, then many traders have picked up in the upward (or downward) trend of an asset and are attempting to make a good return trading its trend. By combining the volume with the highs and lows on the average price candle you should be able to predict the turning point. You can then place a trade which goes against the majority movement in the market and you should see a correspondingly high return as your trade seems riskier than going with the market.

It is vital to consider your trade carefully before placing it; if the volume movement is high; and you have calculated the highs and lows correctly, then timing is crucial. You need to trade just before it peaks and reverses; this will allow you to make the maximum possible return, and, provide a great sense of satisfaction!

DISCERPTION NOTE

This note for you decide how will you write your on-martingale strategy there are more ways to incise your betting volume the details I mention in other chapters

CHAPTER 5

Secret of martingale strategy

In my starting stage of work, I did research that maybe help you to won most of time to achieve amount profit the detail I given below

The amount of deposit 250	When its reach 500	When its reach 1000	When its reach 2000
2	7	10	11
5	15	21	23
11	31	43	47
23	62	86	95
46	125	172	191
93	250	345	383

The red line I never reach notice this is high rick because if you lose money its will go everything. Kindly please ensure that if you lose more than 5 time don't put more money to get back all you lose. Please close your computer and don't trade anymore

this is my personal strategy I used many time and I succeed. I briefly want to share some Kinde of personal stories that I made big mistake its lost everything I have that will be include next chapter

when I used martingale strategy I always use indicator and economics calendar that give me more comfortable trade I never lose more 5 time in a row because if you know that market is moving this way it chance to win the following trade 89% that is good enough to maintain the money management.

Most people have bad attitude if you lose try to follow the losing amount to cover up at-last they lose everything no more balance to trade. I prefer to say that mostly if you want to use the forex market trading most profitable way is knowing the proper economic calendar and indicator

Understand and Respect the Martingale!

Binary options brokers make sure that they have a mathematical edge because that is their business, if you start to look at binary options trading as a business also then you will need to do the same. So, the real question is; how can you get your own mathematical edge? Compounding is one way and what you are about to learn now is another, most people will tell you that any martingale approach is gambling. In fact, let's be realistic, for most people it is gambling, and the next question is being you 'most people'?

Since most people won't understand what is about to follow we are going to have to just call it gambling, many will, and they are entitled to do so. The reality of life is that nothing is guaranteed, and everything is gambling to some extent anyway. If for example you get a job and commit your life to company X, you are gambling on the fact that the company X will not shut down and leave you unemployed, or let you go because they are downsizing. That example is an extremely low risk form of gambling, but gambling nonetheless. Low risk = low rewards, high risk = high rewards!

Since there is no trading system on earth that will win 100% of the time, loss must be calculated in to any profitable trading plan. If you do not yet have a trading method with a high win rate and few consecutive losses, then please visit the Forex Basics and Trading Strategies sections of this website. After that you can grab a Free Membership here, so you can watch the free video course and expand your knowledge further. What is explained in detail throughout those sections and that video course will be taken to new speeds in the Binary Options Strategy lessons that follow.

The Low Risk Martingale in Action

A martingale approach has been around a very long time and you can use it intelligently, or you can use it to gamble. What we are going to do here is to use it intelligently and only to the extent of our means. One of the first things you need to figure out is how many trades you usually take per day on average. If you can sit down for a few hours per day for example, you will need to judge how many trades you are getting on average for those few hours. If you generally keep your eye on the charts all day, then you need an average trade per day for that. Just like the previous lesson your best friend here is experience with your trading method and some trading history to review.

Now you need to think about how many winning trades it would take to erase a loss of your maximum martingale depth. A smart and not too deep place to start with this is a 2-level deep martingale, which means you would need to lose 3 trades in a row to consider the day a loss. The following table shows you the numbers based on an initial trade of some common sizes and we will use 70% payouts for these examples to keep it extreme

70% Return	$10 Start	$25 Start	$50 Start
Martingale 1	$25	$61	$122
Martingale 2	$60	$148	$296
Wins Needed	14	14	14
Losses to Lose	3	3	3
Session Profit/Loss	$95	$234	$468

Update 19.03.11

initial lot 0.05
lot exponen 2
Pip Step 20

AliFx: End of level 1

		1	2	3	4	5	6	7	8	9	10	11
total pip movement		20	40	60	80	100	120	140	160	180	200	220
# of trades		L1	L2	L3	L4	L5	L6	L7	L8	L9	L10	L11
0	0.05	1.00	2.00	3.00	4.00	5.00	6.00	7.00	8.00	9.00	10.00	11.00
1	0.10		2.00	4.00	6.00	8.00	10.00	12.00	14.00	16.00	18.00	20.00
2	0.20			4.00	8.00	12.00	16.00	20.00	24.00	28.00	32.00	36.00
3	0.40				8.00	16.00	24.00	32.00	40.00	48.00	56.00	64.00
4	0.80					16.00	32.00	48.00	64.00	80.00	96.00	112.00
5	1.60						32.00	64.00	96.00	128.00	160.00	192.00
6	3.20							64.00	128.00	192.00	256.00	320.00
7	6.40								128.00	256.00	384.00	512.00
8	12.80									256.00	512.00	768.00
9	25.60										512.00	1024.00
10	51.20											1024.00
		1.00	4.00	11.00	26.00	57.00	120.00	247.00	502.00	1013.00	2036.00	4083.00

Average profit per day = 250 pip
if capital = 50usd, and trade 2 cen, then per day profit = 5usd
then % profit per day = 10%

Safe capital calculation
calculation based on safe level, level 6 (120 pip movement without retrace), ... exclude high impact news

	0.01	0.02	0.03	0.04	0.05	0.06	0.07	0.08	0.09	0.1
Capital	24	48	72	96	120	144	168	192	216	240

Before you proceed with a 2-level deep martingale strategy you will need to be sure that losing 3 trades in a row with your trading method is not very common. It doesn't matter if it happens occasionally, it just matters that it doesn't happen that often. As you can see in the above table it would require 14 wins to erase a 2-level martingale full loss, with an 80% payout the required wins drop to just 11, with an 85% payout it drops to 10. The higher percentage payouts you can find the less wins you will need and the easier your job will be. Visit our Regulated Binary Options Brokers page to discover up to 100% returns and make this even easier. What you need to do now is consider the above information and create for yourself a session, or daily, goal. Every time you sit down you will either lose 3 in a row and then walk away, or you will win 14 trades (or 10 if you are getting 85% payouts, or just 7 on 100% payouts) and it doesn't matter if they are in a row or not. Let's say you are at 12 wins of 14 required and you just need 2 more, the following would get you there and complete your session: loss, loss, win, loss, win. This is the power of the martingale, but it is very important that you have a solid proven trading plan to follow before you consider it.

It is always best to stay as realistic as you can and not assume that you will win every session. The following table helps you understand why you don't have to win every session and what your requirements are to stay profitable

5 Sessions	$95/Session	$234/Session	$468/Session
0 Session Loss	$475	$1170	$2340
1 Session Loss	$285	$702	$1404
2 Session Loss	$95	$234	$468
3 Session Loss	-$95	-$234	-$468
4 Session Loss	-$285	-$702	-$1404
5 Session Loss	-$475	-$1170	-$2340

The numbers are clear and obviously you will prefer not to lose any session, but you could lose 1 of 5 and still be doing quite well. A worst-case scenario for you should be the losing of 2 sessions per 5 which still leaves you with some profit. After that you start heading to negative territory which probably means your trading strategy, or your ability to execute it, is not yet up to speed and you need to get back to studying and practicing for a while longer.

Let's quickly run some more numbers based on the same concept and using the worst-case scenario 70% payouts again.

70% Return	$20 Start	$30 Start	$40 Start
Martingale 1	$49	$73	$97
Martingale 2	$119	$178	$236
Wins Needed	14	14	14
Losses to Lose	3	3	3
Session Profit/Loss	$188	$281	$373

ased on the above table being your session target, let's see how that plays across 5 sessions.

5 Sessions	$188/Session	$281/Session	$373/Session
0 Session Loss	$940	$1405	$1865
1 Session Loss	$564	$843	$1119
2 Session Loss	$188	$281	$373
3 Session Loss	-$188	-$281	-$373
4 Session Loss	-$564	-$843	-$1119
5 Session Loss	-$940	-$1405	-$1865

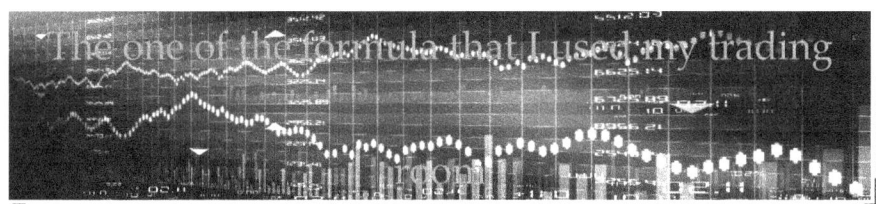

Main Settings

Profit %	Account Size	Max Risk %	Max Risk Value	Start Trade Risk
85%	$1,000	10	$100.00	$12.64

Style A — Low Risk Martingale - 3 Loss in a Row Maximum Per Day

Trade #	Trade Risk	Position Size	Trade Reward	Next Win Rewards
1	$12.64	$23.38	$10.74	$10.74
2	$27.50	$50.88	$23.38	$10.74
3	$59.86	$110.74	$50.88	$10.74

Max Risk= $100.00   Wins Needed= 9.31

Style B — Low Risk Martingale - 3 Loss in a Row Maximum Per Day

Trade #	Rounded	Position Size	Trade Reward	Running Reward
1	$13.00	$12.64	$10.74	$10.74
2	$28.00	$27.50	$23.38	$10.74
3	$60.00	$59.86	$50.88	$10.74

Max Risk= $100.00   Wins Needed= 9.31

Rounded= $101.00   Rounded= 9.00

*Only change the values in the black cells

CHAPTER 6

Indicators mainly using in martingale strategy

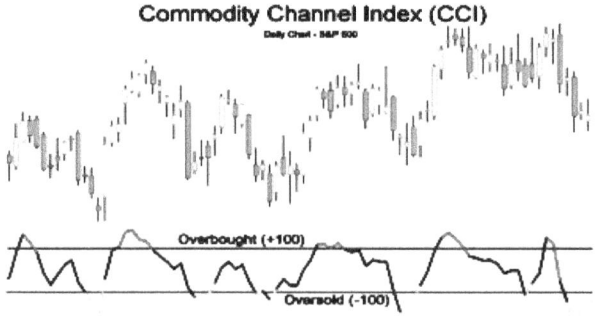

CCI Indicator
The Commodity Channel Index (CCI) is an oscillator originally developed by Donald Lambert and featured in his book "Commodities Channel Index: Tools for Trading Cyclical Trends". Since its introduction, the indicator has grown in popularity and is now a very common tool for traders to identify cyclical trends not only in commodities but also equities and currencies. In this article, we'll look at what exactly the CCI calculates, and how you can apply it to enhance your trading.
Understanding the CCI Like most oscillators, the CCI was developed to determine overbought and oversold levels. The CCI does this by measuring the relation between price and a moving average (MA), or, more specifically, normal deviations from that average. The actual CCI calculation, shown below, illustrates how this measurement is made.

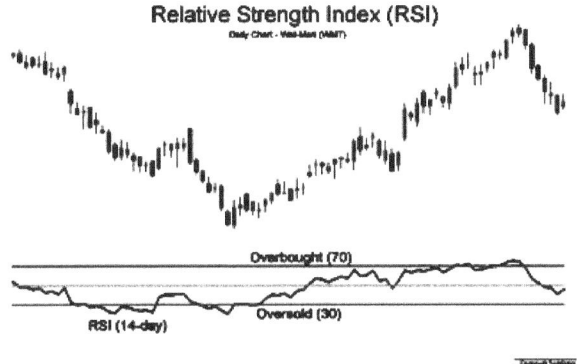

RSI indicator
The Relative Strength Index (RSI), developed by J. Welles Wilder, is a momentum oscillator that measures the speed and change of price movements. The RSI oscillates between zero and 100. Traditionally the RSI is considered overbought when above 70 and oversold when below 30

The smoothing process affects RSI values. RS values are smoothed after the first calculation. Average Loss equals the sum of the losses divided by 14 for the first calculation. Subsequent calculations multiply the prior value by 13, add the most recent value and then divide the total by 14. Trend line indicator

A trendline is a straight line that connects two or more price points. Extending this line into the future, it also acts as a line of support or resistance

CHAPTER 7

Candlesticks / CANDLESTICK PATTERNS

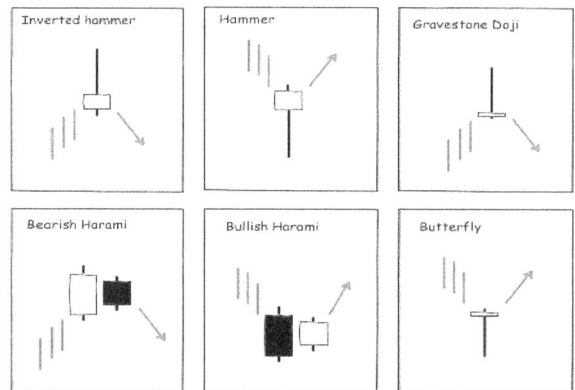

THE MOST PROFITABLE CANDLES THAT TRADERS USE ACCORDING TO MOVING CHART FRAME

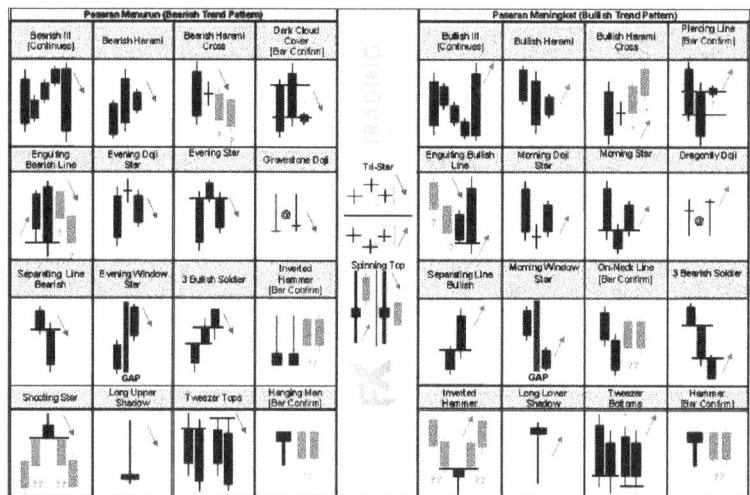

Whether you are new to trading Forex or an old hand at the currency markets, you are likely to share one key aspiration:

How do I become more successful at trading?

One way to improve is to learn by example and to look at some of the most successful Forex traders in the world. In this article, you'll learn about what the top Forex traders in the world have in common and how those strengths helped them to make huge profits.

While you may have heard statistics thrown around suggesting that the ratio of successful Forex traders to unsuccessful ones is small. There are at least a couple of reasons to be sceptical about such claims.

Firstly, hard data is hard to come by on the subject because of the decentralised, over-the-counter nature of the Forex market. But there is plenty of education material and working Forex trading strategies available to better equip your trading performance.

Second, we would expect the distribution of winners and losers to follow something of a bell-curve, meaning that there would be:

very few large losers

a great number of small losers

a great number of small winners; and

very few large winners.

The data that is available from Forex and CFD firms (albeit just a very small slice of the vast global FX market) suggests that the rarest people are very successful traders. Most people stop once they start losing beyond a certain threshold, whereas the big winners keep on trading.

The number of small losers slightly outweighs the number of small winners, mainly because of the effect of market spread. So the percentage of successful Forex traders is not substantially smaller than unsuccessful ones. There is little doubt, though, that the most successful traders are an elite few.

However, by looking at a select group of famous Forex traders we can see that they have a few things in common.

Discipline—the ability to recognise when a trade is wrong and therefore minimise losses.

Risk control—having a strong understanding of a trade's risk/reward. You can read more about this in our risk management guide.

Courage—the willingness to be different from the rest of the crowd, most of the time.

Astuteness—judging how perceptions are shaping market trends.

The upshot of these characteristics has been consistent and large profits.

The world's best Forex trader

Let's begin our review of Forex successful traders by looking at one of the industry's legendary beacons of good fortune, George Soros.

Mr Soros is known as one of the greatest investors in history. He sealed his reputation as a legendary money manager by reportedly profiting more than £1 billion from his short position in pound sterling. He did so ahead of Black Wednesday, 16 September 1992.

At the time, Britain was a part of the Exchange Rate Mechanism (ERM). This mechanism required the government to intervene if the pound weakened beyond a certain level against the Deutsche Mark.

Soros successfully predicted that a combination of circumstances—including the then high level of British interest rates and the unfavourable rate at which Britain had joined the ERM—had left the Bank of England vulnerable.

Britain's commitment to maintaining the pound's value against the Deutsche Mark meant intervening when the pound weakened by either buying sterling or raising interest rates or both. The recession meant that higher interest rates were very painful for the rest of the economy. This hindered investment when encouragement was needed instead.

Economists at the Bank of England recognised that the appropriate level of interest rates was far lower than those required to prop up the pound as part of the ERM. But the value of sterling was maintained because of the UK's public commitment to buying sterling.

In the weeks leading up to Black Wednesday, Soros used his Quantum Fund to build a large position short of sterling. But on the eve of Black Wednesday, comments came from the President of the German Bundesbank. These comments suggested certain currencies could come under pressure.

And this led Soros to increase his position considerably.

When the Bank of England began buying billions of pounds on the Wednesday morning, it found the price of the pound was little moved. This was due to the flood of selling in the market from other speculators following Soros' lead.

A last-ditch attempt to hike UK rates that had briefly hit 15%, proved futile. When the UK announced its exit from the ERM and a resumption of a free-floating pound, the currency plunged 15% against the Deutsche Mark and 25% against the US dollar.

As a result, the Quantum Fund made billions of dollars and Soros became known as the man who broke the Bank of England.

Want to know the best part?

Although Soros' short position in the pound was huge, his downside was always relatively restricted. Leading up to his trade, the market had shown no appetite for sterling strength. This was demonstrated by the repeated need for the British government to intervene in propping up the pound.

Even if his trade had gone wrong and Britain had managed to stay in the ERM, the state of inertia would have more likely prevailed than a large appreciation in the pound.

Here we see Soros' strong appreciation of risk/reward - one of the facets that helped carve his reputation as the best Forex trader in the world. Rather than subscribing to the traditional economic theory that prices will eventually move to a theoretical equilibrium, Soros deems the theory of reflexivity to be more helpful in judging the financial markets.

This theory suggests there is a feedback mechanism between perception and events. In other words, the perceptions of market participants help to shape market prices which in turn reinforce perceptions.

This was played out in his famous sterling short, where the devaluation of the pound only occurred when enough speculators believed the Bank of England could no longer defend its currency.

He once told the Wall Street Journal "I'm only rich because I know when I'm wrong". The quote demonstrates both his willingness to cut a trade that is not working, and the discipline shared by the most successful Forex traders.

Who else counts?

So, George Soros is number 1 on our list as probably the best known of the world's most successful Forex traders and certainly one of the globe's highest earners from a short-term trade.

But who else is up there?

Stanley Druckenmiller

George Soros casts a long shadow and it shouldn't come as too much of a surprise that the most successful Forex trader has ties to another of the names on our list.

Stanley Druckenmiller considers George Soros his mentor. In fact, Mr. Druckenmiller worked alongside him at the Quantum Fund for more than a decade. But Druckenmiller then established a formidable reputation in his own right, successfully managing billions of dollars for his own fund, Duquesne Capital.

As well as being part of Soros' famous Black Wednesday trade, Mr Druckenmiller boasted an incredible record of successive years of double-digit gains with Duquesne before retiring. Druckenmiller's net worth is valued at more than $2 billion.

Druckenmiller says that his trading philosophy for building long-term returns revolves around preserving capital and then aggressively pursuing profits when trades are going well. This approach downplays the importance of being right or wrong.

Instead, it emphasises the value of maximising the opportunity when you are right and minimising the damage when you are wrong. As Druckenmiller said when interviewed for the celebrated book The New Market Wizards, "there are a lot of shoes on the shelf; wear only the ones that fit."

Bill Lipschutz

Oddly enough, Bill Lipschutz made profits numbering in the hundreds of millions of dollars at the FX department of Salomon Brothers in the 1980s - despite no previous experience of the currency markets.

Often called the Sultan of Currencies, Mr Lipschutz describes FX as a very psychological market. And like our other successful Forex traders, the Sultan believes market perceptions help determine price action as much as pure fundamentals.

Lipschutz also agrees with Stanley Druckenmiller's view that how to be a successful trader in Forex, is not dependant on being right more often that you are wrong. Instead, he stresses that you need to work out how to make money when being right only 20 to 30 per cent of the time.

Here's some of Lipschutz's other key tenets.

Any trading idea needs to be well reasoned before you place the trade.

Build a position as the market goes your way and exit the same way.

Then start to ease up once there are signs that the fundamentals and the price action are beginning to change.

There is a need to be aware of the market's focus.

FX is a 24-hour market and doesn't stop moving when you go to bed.

Lipschutz also stresses the need to manage risk, saying that your trading size should be chosen to avoid being forced out of your position if your timing is inexact.

How successful is a successful Forex trader?

We've looked at the biggest Forex successful traders, but there is an army of profitable traders out there. Joining the list of people who can consistently turn a profit each month trading FX, is an achievable goal.

So, what's the bottom line?

Well, even the most successful trader had to begin somewhere and if you can regularly generate profits - you can consider yourself a successful Forex trader.

Hopefully this article has given you some insights into traits shared by the most successful Forex traders. Now maybe you should try to top the Forex trader's list yourself, by participating in our Forex Ball demo contest.

ALL IT TOOK WAS A $12,000 INHERITANCE FROM HIS GRANDMOTHER…THAT WAS THE START TO MAKE HIM FILTHY RICH (Bill Lipschutz)

This is one man who would be very thankful to have had lovely grandmother. But on the other side is a bit funny too…Imagine spending 5 years of your life studying at university for a degree and then leaving the degree collecting dust on the shelf and now you are doing something entirely different from what you studied for?

Wouldn't that be crazy? Well, not according this this story. You see, if that man above had taken the path of his degree, he wouldn't be a billionaire today.

Who is this man? Well, Bill Lipschutz is your man!

You see, Bill Lipschutz was studying to be an architecture in Cornell University when his grandmother died leaving him a portfolio of shares of around $12,000. Bill sold all of it and used this money as his risk capital to start trading the stock market whilst he was still a student.

He started trading the stock market using this money and years later when he started working for Salomon Brothers, he started trading the Forex market.

But here's the thing, Bill Lipschutz eventually graduated, not with one degree but two degrees.

How?

Well, he got his architectural degree, but he also ended up studying a lot of business courses and ended up getting and M.B.A. The thing was, he never practiced as an architect. It was his second degree that paved his way to secure a job with Salomon Brothers.

Bill Lipschutz said that he never remembers deciding to be a trader.

The thing was he did not want to be an architect. It was a gradual process until trading literally took over his life.

What happened to the $12,000 trading account?

Well, he increased it to $250,000 in 4-5 years. But a bad trading decision he made cost him dearly. That $250,000 account which took 4-5 years to build up was blown up in a couple of days. That huge loss was a very important learning experience for him.

There is no clear information of what Bill Lipschutz net worth is currently, but I wouldn't be surprised it would be up there in the hundreds of millions of dollars.

Bill Lipschutz is also reputed to have made $6 million dollars in 6 hours trading the New Zealand Dollar in September 1985 with one of his co-workers/trader.

In other spectacular trade, he made $20 million trading the Japanese yen in 1987.

Also, there was on trade in 1988 where was short on D-Mark by $3 billion (The official currency of Germany until it adopted the euro in 2002. D-mark is an abbreviation of Deutsche Mark).

He was caught out (on the wrong side) and with no liquidity during the New York Trading Session when the Dollar started increasing against the D-Mark and he couldn't bail out of his large short position and when price went up by 1%, he was in deep freaking trouble.

To put this in perspective: one percent of $3billion is $30million. So, Bill Lipschutz was staring at a $30million loss in just 8minutes! At one point during that trading session, that loss started to increase, and he was staring at a $90 million loss. Eventually he managed to close off this trade with an $18million loss for the day during the Tokyo Session came and the dollar started sliding down.

Compared to the $90 million loss, that $18 million loss seemed like a winner.

This was a guy that was trading huge contracts that sometimes moving the currency markets just by his huge orders.

What's the lesson here? there are many people in this life that end up going to universities just to get educated and get a degree and then don't even end up doing the jobs that they were educated for. And there may be many reason for that. But here's the thing: if it's not in your heart, you won't last long. Sometimes it may take a while before someone finally figures out what he wants to do in life.

Bill Lipschultz's net worth is unknown but here's what Wikipedia had to say about how much he was making whilst working for Salomon's Brothers:

He was amongst the top five of all Forex traders worldwide. By 1985, Lipschutz was making $300 million per year for Salomon Brothers.

HE TURNED $2,000 INTO MILLIONS (JACK SCHWAGER)

I can't find a picture of this guy! Honestly! So, if you find a picture, please let me know.

I bet you've never heard of this millionaire trader. And maybe it's for a good reason because this guy likes to maintain a low profile (that's why I can find a picture). But here's the thing: If there's any futures trader who can take $2000 and turn it into a million, Randy McKay would be the one.

An excerpt in The New Market Wizards by Jack Schwager, from Randy McKay:

"In 1970, I returned from a tour in Vietnam. Since I didn't finish school before I left for Vietnam, I needed a job that would allow me to go to school at the same time. My brother, Terry, was a floor broker on the Chicago Mercantile Exchange. He got me a job as a runner on the floor, which allowed me to work in the morning, attend school in the afternoon, and study in the evening.

I worked as a runner for a couple of years with absolutely no intention of getting into this business. I was studying to be a clinical psychologist. Just as I was finishing college, in 1972, the CME launched a subdivision, the International Monetary Market to trade currencies. When the exchange started the IMM division, they sold seats for only $10,000 to try to get bodies into these new trading pits and gave away free seats to all existing members.

As a member, my brother had no need for this seat at the asked me if I'd like to use it in the interim. He gave me the use of the seat and lent me $5,000. I put $3,000 in the bank to pay my living expenses, and used the $2,000 for my trading account."

In the first seven months of trading, he turned that $2,000 into $70,000. And each year he continued to make more money than the previous year. And he was trading in the trading floors at that time.

Then one day he decided to leave the trading floors and start trading from home. By his second year from trading from home, he made his first $1 million.

And tell you what? He continued to increase his trading account every year until 1986 when he suffered his first trading loss for the year.

If there's anybody who would get a medal for consistency in trading, it would be Randy McKay. It's been reported that Randy McKay has been profitable for his own trading account 18 out of 20 years.

Not much is known about Randy Mckay's net worth, but one thing is for sure: it won't be under $10million.

What the lesson here? Well, you can turn $2,000 trading account into $70,000 if you are consistent like cutting your losses and making more than you lose.

THE 5 MOST POWERFUL CANDLESTICK PATTERNS

Candlestick charts are a technical tool that pack data for multiple time frames into single price bars. This makes them more useful than traditional open-high, low-close bars (OHLC) or simple lines that connect the dots of closing prices. Candlesticks build patterns that predict price direction once completed. Proper color coding adds depth to this colorful technical tool, which dates to 18th century Japanese rice traders.

Steve Nison brought candlestick patterns to the Western world in his popular 1991 book, "Japanese Candlestick Charting Techniques." Many traders can now identify dozens of these formations, which have colorful names like bearish dark cloud cover, evening star and three black crows. In addition, single bar patterns including the doji and hammer have been incorporated into dozens of long- and short-side trading strategies. (For related reading, see Candlestick Charting: What Is It?)

Candlestick Pattern Reliability

Not all candlestick patterns work equally well. Their huge popularity has lowered reliability because they've been deconstructed by hedge funds and their algorithms. These well-funded players rely on lightning-speed execution to trade against retail and traditional fund managers who execute technical analysis strategies found in popular texts. In other words, hedge fund managers use software to trap participants looking for high-odds bullish or bearish outcomes. However, reliable patterns continue to appear, allowing for short- and long-term profit opportunities. (See also: The Multiple Strategies of Hedge Funds.

)
Here are five candlestick patterns that perform exceptionally well as precursors of price direction and momentum. Each works within the context of surrounding price bars in predicting higher or lower prices. They are also time sensitive in two ways. First, they only work within the limitations of the chart being reviewed, whether intraday, daily, weekly or monthly. Second, their potency decreases rapidly three to five bars after the pattern has completed.

Top 5 Candlestick Patterns

This analysis relies on the work of Thomas Bulkowski, who built performance rankings for candlestick patterns in his 2008 book, "Encyclopedia of Candlestick Charts." He offers statistics for two kinds of expected pattern outcomes: reversal and continuation. Candlestick reversal patterns predict a change in price direction, while continuation patterns predict an extension in the current price direction.

In the following examples, the hollow white candlestick denotes a closing print higher than the opening print, while the black candlestick denotes a closing print lower than the opening print. (See The Basic Language of Candlestick Charting for more information.)

THREE LINE STRIKE

The bullish three line strike reversal pattern carves out three black candles within a downtrend. Each bar posts a lower low and closes near the intrabar low. The fourth bar opens even lower but reverses in a wide-range outside bar that closes above the high of the first candle in the series. The opening print also marks the low of the fourth bar. According to Bulkowski, this reversal predicts higher prices with an 84% accuracy rate.

TWO BLACK GAPPING

The bearish two black gapping continuation pattern appears after a notable top in an uptrend, with a gap down that yields two black bars posting lower lows. This pattern predicts that the decline will continue to even lower lows, perhaps triggering a broader-scale downtrend. According to Bulkowski, this pattern predicts lower prices with a 68% accuracy rate.

THREE BLACK CROWS

The bearish three black crows reversal pattern starts at or near the high of an uptrend, with three black bars posting lower lows that close near intrabar lows. This pattern predicts that the decline will continue to even lower lows, perhaps triggering a broader-scale downtrend. The most bearish version starts at a new high (point A on the chart) because it traps buyers entering momentum plays. According to Bulkowski, this pattern predicts lower prices with a 78% accuracy rate. (For related reading, see How Do I Build a Profitable Trading Strategy When Spotting a Three Black Crows Pattern?)

EVENING STAR

The bearish evening star reversal pattern starts with a tall white bar that carries an uptrend to a new high. The market gaps higher on the next bar, but fresh buyers fail to appear, yielding a narrow range candlestick. A gap down on the third bar completes the pattern, which predicts that the decline will continue to even lower lows, perhaps triggering a broader-scale downtrend. According to Bulkowski, this pattern predicts lower prices with a 72% accuracy rate. (See also: How Is an Evening Star Pattern Interpreted by Analysts and Traders?)

ABANDONED BABY

The bullish abandoned baby reversal pattern appears at the low of a downtrend, after a series of black candles print lower lows. The market gaps lower on the next bar, but fresh sellers fail to appear, yielding a narrow range doji candlestick with opening and closing prints at the same price.

A bullish gap on the third bar completes the pattern, which predicts that the recovery will continue to even higher highs, perhaps triggering a broader-scale uptrend. According to Bulkowski, this pattern predicts higher prices with a 70% accuracy rate. (For more, see Using Bullish Candlestick Patterns to Buy Stocks.)

The Bottom Line
Candlestick patterns capture the attention of market players, but many reversal and continuation signals emitted by these patterns don't work reliably in the modern electronic environment. Fortunately, statistics by Thomas Bulkowski show unusual accuracy for a narrow selection of these patterns, offering traders actionable buy and sell signals.

HE COULD HAVE BEEN KILLED DURING WORLD WAR II BY THE NAZIS

If there was one trader who was born at the wrong place at the wrong time, but somehow ended up being the 29th richest person in the world with a new worth **$24.2 billion** as of April 2015 according to Forbes.

I don't think there is any trader out there that can break the record of this man who made more than $1 billion dollars in profit in one single day!

Perhaps one of the biggest misconceptions that most people seem to have about professional traders is that they are ultra-smart Ivy-League math-wiz's who have some super-human ability to make money in the markets. Maybe he has the same power that make him billionaire, but smart and knowledge trader always win because they know where to stop what need to do when they stuck in losses.

They stop trading in that day. Wait for best signal maybe 2 hours might be more.

That guy is called George Soros.

Here is his brief story:

- He was born in 1930 in Budapest and survived the Nazi occupation of Hungary during World War II. Seriously, those bloody Nazis could have killed him!
- Anyway, he left the war-torn Budapest and managed to make his way to England and Graduated in London School of Economics in 1952.
- In 1956, he emigrated to USA and later he took a job working as a financial analyst and trader in New York.
- In September of 1992, George Soros risked $10 billion on a single currency speculation when he shorted the British pound.
- His bet was right, and in a single day the trade generated a profit of $1 billion – ultimately, it was reported that his profit on the transaction almost reached $2 billion.
- Because of this he is often referred to as "the man who broke the Bank of England."

What made George Soros so successful in taking large bets like that that made him billions?

Well, here's your answer:

- George Soros was a master at translating broad-brush economic trends into highly leveraged, killer plays in bonds and currencies.

-
- As an investor, Soros was a short-term speculator, making huge bets on the directions of financial markets.
- He believed that financial markets can best be described as chaotic.
- The prices of securities and currencies depend on human beings, or the traders – both professional and non-professional – who buy and sell these assets. These persons often act out based on emotion, rather than logical considerations.
- He also believed that market participants influenced one another and moved in herds.
- He said that most of the time he moved with the herd, but always watched for an opportunity to get out in front and "make a killing."

How could he tell when the time was right?

Soros has said that he would have an instinctive physical reaction about when to buy and sell, making is strategy a difficult model to emulate.

So, if you think there is a trading strategy that George Soros uses, and you've been searching for it the forget it! What's the lesson here?

- It does not matter what country or what conditions you faced in life as a child growing up.
-
- If you have a little bit of decent education and saw an opportunity to make money of that knowledge and you work hard, you'd get somewhere, just like George Soros did.

THE NERDY TRADER WHO MADE MILLIONS BY USING COMPUTER TRADING PROGRAMS

Now, not much is known about how much this guy shown above net worth is, but it should be in the multi millions I believe.

His name is Ed Seykota.

He is a commodities trader, who earned S.B. degrees in Electrical Engineering from MIT and Management from the MIT Sloan School of Management, both in 1969. He is reported to be the first to conceive and develop the first commercial computerized trading systems.

You make rightfully call him the computer nerd who became a multi-million-dollar trader.

Not much is currently known about is net worth but if rumours are true, he certainly deserves to be called a trading success story.

What's the lesson here? Computers can do your trading. You just must find the right system and code it and watch it churn in billions! (just kidding). But on a serious note, yes, you can make money by using computer programs which trade on your behalf but the important thing in my opinion is to use the right trading method that works in each currency pair.

HE WAS ONCE A TAXI CAB DRIVER BUT NOW HE'S WORTH $5 BILLION

If you are a taxi driver and thought you can never become a billionaire, well, you should be motivated to know that there was once a person like who driving taxis to make a living and his net

Bruce Kovner

worth is now $5 Billion according to Forbes April 2015!

And just to think that there are some people alive today that have been taxied around by this billionaire trader? Well…he wasn't actually a billionaire back then, but he was a taxi driver.

He had some turbulent childhood as well and it must be tough for him as His mother committed suicide.

He started trading with $3,000 and used that to trade the soybeans futures contract and that trade saw him made a paper profit of $40,000 and then when his profits started to drop, he bailed out with only $23,000. He panicked and sold it. He said that the was a good lesson for him in risk management.

Who is this man? It's Bruce Kovner.

As of Feb 2017, Bruce Kovner's Net Worth is $5 Billion. Not bad for a former taxi driver.

What's the lesson here? Well, it does not matter what kind of job you are doing right now. Give a shot a trading. You never know where you will end up in the end. Your past career/job does not determine who you will be in the future.

HE WAS A STREET SELLER…A KID WHO GREW UP SELLING NEWSPAPERS, MAGAZINES, COCA-COLA AND BUBBLE GUM DOOR TO DOOR WHO BECAME THE WORLD'S BEST INVESTOR

Warren Buffet

From an early age, he showed great interest in making and saving money…and that later translated to making him billions and many millions of dollars to many of those investors that invested with his company. You probably won't recognize him from his childhood photos with his two sisters above. But you know what? His net worth now is $73.6 Billion as of Feb 2017 according for Forbes.
That kid above, who is now a insanely rich old man today is Warren Buffet!
Here's an excerpt from Forbes:
Warren Buffett is wealthier than ever thanks to the stellar performance of his diversified holding company, Berkshire Hathaway. Its coveted Class A stock, which is the most expensive of any public U.S. company, eclipsed $200,000 per share for the first time in August 2014. Buffett moved to 3rd richest on Forbes' 2015 list of the worlds' richest, up 4th richest in 2014.
With dozens of subsidiaries, including in railroads, insurance and energy, Berkshire Hathaway posted $182 billion in 2013 revenue and $19.5 billion in net income. Still inking big deals, Buffett's Berkshire Hathaway bought battery maker Duracell from Procter & Gamble in November 2014 for $4.7 billion.
A generous philanthropist, he bested his own giving record in July 2014, giving away Berkshire shares worth $2.8 billion, primarily to the Bill & Melinda Gates Foundation but also to his children's foundations, bringing his lifetime giving to nearly $23 billion.
Buffett says his best ever investment was buying Benjamin Graham's book "The Intelligent Investor" in 1949. He later studied under Graham before moving home to Nebraska and acquiring a struggling textiles company in 1962, Berkshire Hathaway. In early February 2015, it was the fourth most valuable public company in the U.S. with a market capitalization of $355 billion.

THE TRADING FLOOR CLERK WHO LATER BECAME A BILLIONAIRE TRADER

Paul Tudor Jones

He currently has a net worth of $4.7 Billion as of Feb 2017 according to Forbes. He was born in Memphis, Tennessee. He finished high school and went on to University of Virginia, earning an undergraduate degree in economics in 1976 as well as his college welterweight boxing championship.

In 1976, he started working on the trading floors as a clerk. Then later he became a broker. In 1980, he went strictly on his own for two and a half profitable years, before he "really got bored".

I mean, seriously? Did he get bored making money?

Anyway…as the story goes: out of his boredom, he wanted to try something different: he then applied to Harvard Business School, was accepted, and was packed up and ready to go when he thought to himself: "this is crazy, because for what I'm doing here, they're not going to teach me anything like this in Harvard. This skill set is not something that they teach in business school."

How right he was! Who is this guy? Its Paul Tudor Jones.

He was advised to go down to New Orleans to talk with commodity broker Eli Tullis, who hired and then mentored him in trading cotton futures at the New York Cotton Exchange. And this is what Jones later said:

"Eli Tullis was the toughest son of a bitch I ever knew. He taught me that trading is very competitive, and you have to be able to handle getting your butt kicked. No matter how you cut it, there are enormous emotional ups and downs involved."

That was just the beginning. Years later, he was a billionaire trader. What a story!

HE CAME FROM VERY HUMBLE BEGINNINGS…THIS TRADER MADE $3.7 BILLION IN A SINGLE YEAR IN 2007.

John Paulson

This guy's net worth is $11.2 Billion as of April 2015 according to Forbes. He really came from humble beginnings.

Some people make a fortune in crisis. As a matter of fact, times of crises present great opportunities for wealth creation…that is, if you are prepared for it. This guy was definitely prepared. This guy made $3.7 billion during the 2007 Mortgage Crisis.

He is John Paulson.

His prominence and fortune were made in 2007 when he earned $3.7 billion personally and was transformed "from an obscure money manager into a financial legend" by using credit default swaps to effectively bet against the U.S. subprime mortgage lending market.

In 2011, Paulson earned "$4.9 billion" according to Business Insider.

How did he make his fortune in 2007?

Here's how: he made a bet on the sub-prime mortgage crash in 2007 by betting against four out of the five biggest British Banks, many called it the greatest trade ever made. It made him a billionaire, making $3.7bn in a single year

Somebody else misfortune became his fortune.

THE HIGH SCHOOL POKER PLAYER WHO BECAME A BILLIONAIRE TRADER

This trader played poker as a high school kid. In fact, he said that playing poker taught him a good lesson about taking risks. Risks can kill you or make you wealthy and for his case, it made him

Steven Cohen

very rich.
Who is this guy? Its Steven Cohen.
He opened up his first brokerage account with $1,000 of his own tuition money. At 22 he got a job as a junior trader for Gronstal & Co and on his first day he made $8,000. That was pretty much the star of his rise to become one of the world's billionaire traders. Guess what his net worth is? Stephen Cohen's net worth is $13 Billion as of Feb 2017 according to Forbes.
I bet there aren't many former poker players worth as much as this guy is! Good on him!

THIS TRADER HAS HIS GRANDMOTHER TO BLAME FOR HIS BILLIONS!

Edward Lampert

There are many stories of grandmother's wrong influence on children. And this guy is no exception. In fact, his grandmother is to be blamed for this guy's net worth as of Feb 2017 is $1.96 Billion! You see, his grandmother was a passive investor and big fan of Louis Rukeyser's Wall Street Week television program. She instilled in him an interest in investing. His mother would later recall that young boy would sit with his grandmother reviewing and evaluating the performance of her stock picks in the daily newspaper.
And that's how Edward Lampert got hooked in trading as they say: "the rest is history."
So, listen, mums and dads, it's better to have your kids around grandmas and grandpas who can instil them an interest in investing. It may not only be in the areas of investing but in other areas in the life of you children to become respectable and successful men and women when they grow up.

HE STARTED TRADING IN HIS HARVARD SCHOOL DORM WHILE STILL A STUDENT

Kenneth Griffin

This guy's net worth is $7.7 billion according to Forbes in Feb 2017. Who is he? Ken Griffin.
This is what Wikipedia has to say about this man:
In 1986, Griffin started to invest during his freshman year at Harvard University after reading a Forbes magazine article. During his second year at Harvard, he started a hedge fund focused on convertible bond arbitrage.
The fund was capitalized with $265,000 from friends and family, including money from his grandmother. He installed a satellite link to his dorm to acquire real-time market data. The investment strategy helped preserve capital during the stock market crash of 1987. Griffin's early success enabled him to launch a second fund, and between the two funds he was managing just over $1 million. Griffin graduated from Harvard in 1989 with a degree in economics.
Those were the beginnings to making billions of years later.

HE WAS ONCE HOT DOG STAND SELLER IN COLLEGE AND A UNIVERSITY PHD DROP OUT, BUT NOW IS WORTH BILLION$

Stanley Drunken miller

This guy's net worth as of Feb 2017 according to Forbes is $4.7 Billion. He is Stanley Drunken miller.
This is what Wikipedia had to say about him:
He grew up in a middle-class household in the suburbs of Philadelphia. His parents divorced when he was in elementary school and he went to live with his father in Gibbstown, New Jersey and then in Richmond, Virginia (his sisters, Helen and Salley, would stay with their mother in Philadelphia).

Drunken miller is a graduate of Collegiate School, Richmond, Virginia. In 1975, he received a BA in English and economics from Bowdoin College (where he opened a hot dog stand with Lawrence B. Lindsey, who later became economic policy adviser to President George W. Bush).

He dropped out of a three-year Ph.D. program in economics at the University of Michigan in the middle of the second semester to accept a position as an oil analyst for Pittsburgh National Bank.

In 1988, he was hired by George Soros to his Quantum Fund. He and Soros famously "broke the Bank of England" when they shorted British pound sterling in 1992, reputedly making more than $1 billion in profits. They reasoned out that the Bank of England did not have enough foreign currency reserves with which to buy enough sterling to prop up the currency and that raising interest rates would be politically unsustainable

Here's what Forbes had to say about him:

Famed investor Stan Drunken miller was George Soros' main man when together they "broke the Bank of England," earning a $1 billion profit by shorting the pound in 1992.

Born in a middle-class home in Pittsburgh, Pennsylvania, Drunken miller attended Bowdoin College and pursued a PhD at the University of Michigan.

He eventually dropped out and went to work for Pittsburgh National Bank. After becoming head of equity research, Drunken miller left to launch the legendary Duquesne Capital Management, a hedge fund he ran until 2010, when he reconverted it into a family office. While running Duquesne, Drunken miller had stints at Dreyfus and with George Soros

I hope these real trading success stories from those who are real millionaires (and billionaires) are enough to get you excited that you CAN DO THIS.

Just go through my list of 7-way successful traders approach trading and make sure you take it to heart

DISCERPTION NOTE

....
....
....
....
....
....
....
....
....
....
....
....
....
....
....
....
....
....
....
....
....
....
....
....
....
....
....

This describe you experience and mention you daily profit details check daily your writing before start trading. One Last Thing…

TRADE NOTE

....
....
....
....
....
....
....
....
....
....
....
....
....
....
....
....
....
....
....
....
....
....
....
....
....
....
....
....
.... write your own note with new strategy you found that you make profit

.... This is your behavior therapy write your loss and when did you stop trading(last amount) next day starting entry

....
....
....
....
....
....
....
....
....
....
....
....
....
....
....
....
....
....
....
....
....
....
....
....
....
......................make your daily chart with trend line

..........................which indicator you learn and how it's works.

..........................what did you learn from martingale strategy did you trade after 5 loss.

....
....
....
....
....
....
....
....
....
....
....
....
....
....
....
....
....
....
....
....
....
....
....
....
....
....
.........................."The note is yours "

....
....
....
....
....
....
....
....
....
....
....
....
....
....
....
....
....
....
....
....
....
....
....
....
....
....
........................." The note is yours

A BRIEF HISTORY OF FOREX

Bretton Woods 1944. USD Becomes the World's Reserve Currency.

In July 1944, with the Second World War still raging in Europe and South-East Asia, 730 representatives from the 44 Allied nations convened at the Mount Washington Hotel in Bretton, New Hampshire, USA, for the United Nations Monetary and Financial Conference. Bretton Woods was an attempt to reach a consensus on how to govern the international economy in the aftermath of the war, as well as to address the isolationist policies of economic discrimination and trade warfare, which many believed had contributed to both World Wars, as well as to the Great Depression. As such, eradicating what had come to be known as "beggar thy neighbour policies" (policies that alleviate a country's economic woes at the expense of other countries), and encouraging a freer flow of trade between nations, became a focal point for the conference. Essential to the agreement was an international system of payments to facilitate trade with safeguards in place to prevent large fluctuations in currency value or competitive devaluations. For all these reasons Bretton Woods was a major milestone in the development of the foreign exchange market, and indeed the global financial system we have today.

It was the first time a comprehensive monetary system had been negotiated between nation states, and even though most of the key points of the Bretton Woods system have since been abandoned, its legacy lives on in the institutions it gave rise to. The agreement that was reached at Bretton Woods on the 22nd of July 1944 led to the creation of the International Monetary Fund (IMF), the International Bank for Reconstruction and Development (now part of the World Bank) and the General Agreement on Tariffs and Trade (GATT).

Key to the Bretton Woods agreement was a system of fixed exchange rates between countries whose currency values were all pegged to the U.S dollar, and the US dollar's convertibility to gold at a fixed rate of $35 dollars per ounce. This effectively made the US dollar the world's reserve currency as it took on the role that gold had formerly played under the gold standard. In addition to becoming the world's currency, it's interchangeability with gold made it the currency with the highest purchasing power. Also, the way other currencies were pegged to it, each with its own fixed rate, meant that the majority of international transactions were denominated in US dollars. Taking into account that in the wake of WWII the European powers most affected by the conflict were also heavily in debt to the United States, the geopolitical and economic climate was absolutely ideal for the rise of the United States as the world's superpower. While Britain had been the dominant economic force in the 19th and early 20th century, with the sterling taking pride of place as the world's reserve currency during this period, the second half of the twentieth century would see dominance passing to the United States.

Post Bretton Woods. The Rise of Free Market Capitalism.

Bretton Woods would last until 1971, at which point it was superseded by the short-lived Smithsonian agreement brokered by US President Richard Nixon. However, the golden age of Bretton Woods only really lasted until 1968, up until this time there was a steady improvement in global production and trade, and from 1959 onwards all currencies that were part of the agreement enjoyed full convertibility. But it was the dollar's relationship to gold that would prove to be the real problem that would eventually unhinge the system, this and the fact that the United States was running a large balance of payments deficit to help fund European recovery and keep the financial system liquid. Economists foresaw this eventuality more than a decade in advance, and indeed the problem of keeping gold at $35 per ounce was a real issue as far back as the late 1950's.

The main problem with Bretton Woods was perhaps best stated in 1960 by Robert Triffin, an economist who wrote of what would later come to be known as Triffin's Dilemma. Simply put, Triffin's Dilemma stated that the US deficit was vital to economic growth and to the liquidity of the financial system, but that eventually the very deficit that was aiding Europe's post-war recovery was bound to undermine confidence in the US dollar as the World's reserve currency, and could eventually lead to widespread financial instability.

The US dollar was the only currency that enjoyed gold convertibility, and at the end of the Second World War the US held around 65% of the world's gold reserves. However, inflation had led to it not being economically viable to produce much more gold, and as more and more US dollars flooded into the global financial system, and US gold reserves hardly budged, dollar confidence started to wane as it became apparent that the US would be unable to meet its commitments should dollar holders desire to enforce dollar convertibility. Also, the fact that there was a free market on which gold was traded (separate from the transactions conducted by central banks under Bretton Woods rates), led to a situation where it was cheaper to buy gold at the Bretton Woods rate and then sell it on to the open market. By 1971 the US only held enough gold to cover 22% of foreign US dollar reserves and was running a $56 billion reserve deficit. Add to this the country's growing public debt which was being used to fund the Great Society initiatives introduced by President Lyndon B. Johnson, as well as the on-going Vietnam War, and it became clear that the Bretton Woods system had become untenable.

In November of 1967 the U.K devalued the sterling from $2.80 to $2.40. In November of 1968 an exchange crisis led to the close of the French, German and British markets. In August of 1968 the French franc was devalued from 0.18 grams of gold per franc to 0.16 grams. In October of the same year the German Deutsche mark was revalued from $0.25 to $0.273. Finally, in May of 1971 the Deutsche mark and the Dutch guilder were floated. On August 15th, 1971, US President Richard Nixon withdrew US dollar gold convertibility as well as imposing a 10% import duty and temporarily locking down wages and prices. This came to be known as the Nixon Shock and caused all major economic powers except France to float their currencies and begin intervening by buying up dollars. In December of 1971 the Smithsonian Agreement was signed by the G-10 countries. It was an attempt to keep the Bretton Woods system alive by adjusting its fixed rates to more accurately reflect the market pressures of the early 1970s. The dollar was re-pegged to gold at the new price of $38 per ounce and was allowed to fluctuate within a range of 2.25%, rather than the 1% range permitted by Bretton Woods, with other nations agreeing to readjust their fixed rates to the newly devalued dollar accordingly.

The biggest difference the Smithsonian Agreement had to Bretton Woods was that the US dollar was no-longer to be convertible to gold. While the Smithsonian agreement adjusted the relationships between the world's currencies, it did not address the fundamental imbalances that had led to the dollar's devaluation in the first place. The US continued to run a huge deficit, as well as increasing its money supply at an inflationary rate, this led to other central banks being forced to intervene in order to keep their own currencies from appreciating, pegged as they were to the dollar at a fixed rate. By 1972 the sterling was finally allowed to float against the dollar. A rise in the value of gold led to the dollar having to be revalued again in February of 1972 at $42.22 per ounce (causing all major currencies to also revalue against the dollar). By March of the same year, after huge interventions by European central banks costing around $3.5 billion, the fixed rate system collapsed entirely and the value of the US dollar was henceforth to be determined by free market economics.

OPEC and the Oil Crisis of '73.

Up until now we have overlooked a significant player in our story. If gold features heavily in the history of Forex, then oil, as vital to the wheels of industry as it is precious, certainly deserves a section of its own. To say that free market capitalism as we now know it would not have been possible were it not for oil is not to overstate the case. Gold may have enjoyed a period where it was the backbone of the international monetary system, but the growth of our global economy was literally and figuratively driven by oil.

America's late entry into the Second World War, its financial standing thereafter, and its status as reserve currency with the signing of Bretton Woods, are often cited as contributing factors for its rise to superpower status. But the United States didn't just emerge from WWII relatively unscathed, with much of Europe indebted to it, and its currency central to the global monetary system; the rise of the United States also coincided with the discovery of its own oil reserves, which quickly replaced coal as the country's primary source of energy. Just as the 19th century belonged to the British Empire; an empire, it should be noted, powered by coal. The 20th century would belong to the United States, and would be the century of oil.

As a backdrop to the events that we have already looked at, it's important to keep in mind that the post WWII years saw an ever-increasing demand for oil. Between the end of the Second World War and the demise of the Smithsonian Agreement the global consumption of oil tripled, and the demand for it increased more than fivefold. After WWII oil was rapidly replacing coal; it was abundant, cheap, easier to transport than coal, and also conferred a competitive advantage in terms of productivity to countries that opted to make the switch. Millions upon millions of barrels flowed out of the Middle East and Venezuela, fuelling post war reconstruction, economic recovery and global growth.

Oil's widespread uptake also had the effect of gradually shifting the balance of power, making many countries increasingly reliant on a constant affordable supply from oil-producing nations. The first time the members of the Organisation of Arab Petroleum Exporting Countries (OPEC) attempted to employ what came to be known as the "oil weapon" was early in June of 1967, a day after the start of the Six Day War. In response to an Israeli incursion into Egyptian, Jordanian and Syrian territories OPEC members issued an oil embargo against all countries deemed to be in support of Israel and within days the Arab oil supply had been reduced by around 60%. The situation threatened to worsen when civil war broke out in Nigeria the following month, removing a further 500,000 barrels of crude oil from the global supply chain each day. This first oil embargo would be short-lived and largely unsuccessful due to the existence of relatively healthy reserves, as well as the re-routing of supplies to areas most affected by the embargo. However, OPEC's second attempt at throwing its weight around would have a much more destabilising effect.

Between 1967 and 1973 the global economy's reliance on cheap oil had reduced surplus capacity to dangerously low levels. In 1970, there were around 3 million barrels of surplus capacity per day (excluding the U.S), by 1973 this had shrank to 500,000 barrels per day. So when OPEC wielded the "oil weapon" for the second time on October 17th 1973, the stakes would be significantly higher than they were in 1967. A number of convergent factors contributed to the oil crisis of '73. Tense negotiations between OPEC and Western oil companies regarding pricing and production had been on-going for some time. Also, when in 1971 President Richard Nixon put an end to the Bretton Woods system by withdrawing the US dollar's convertibility to gold, the inevitable US dollar devaluation which ensued affected oil-producing countries because oil was (and still is) priced in US dollars. Add to this the fact that US oil production peaked at around 10 million barrels per day in 1970 (declining steadily thereafter), and that by 1973 the US was actually importing 6 million barrels per day, making it extremely vulnerable to disruptions in supply, and you have the ideal conditions for a perfect storm.

On the 6th of October 1973, during the Jewish holy day of Yom Kippur, Egypt and Syria invaded Israeli territories that had been seized by Israel during the Six Day War six years earlier. On October 17th, in response to US support of Israel during the conflict, OPEC raised the price of oil by 70%, as well as imposing an embargo against the United States and any other countries that had supported Israel during the conflict. The war would be over by the end of October, but OPEC refused to change its course. In November of the same year OPEC cut oil production by 25%, and threatened a further 5% cut. In December the price of oil was again doubled. By January, when Israel agreed to pull its troops back to the east side of the Suez Canal, the price of oil was four times higher than it had been before the crisis began.

The attitude of the oil-producers during this period can be summed up by a memorable quote from the Shah of Iran that was publicised by the New York Times in December of 1973:

"Of course [the price of oil] is going to rise… Certainly!... You [the West] increased the price of wheat you sell us by 300%, and the same for sugar and cement… You buy our crude oil and sell it back to us, refined as petrochemicals, at a hundred times the price you've paid to us… It's only fair that, from now on, you should pay more for oil. Let's say ten times more."

Iran had not participated in the embargo, continuing to ship oil to the West throughout the conflict, but it was clear that the age of cheap oil was over and everybody knew it.

The oil crisis changed the geopolitical landscape and the global economy in many key ways. The inflated prices at which OPEC nations were selling their oil after the embargo caused economic growth to slow in the West while also causing inflation, a situation that came to be known as "stagflation". Also, the quadrupling of the price of oil immediately led to a huge flow of capital from the West to the oil-exporting nations of the Middle-East, a great deal of which was spent on weapons and technology, further exacerbating tensions in the region and leading to an increased American military presence.

The price of oil, as well as its consistent supply, began to figure heavily in the agendas of industrialised nations, such was the shock caused by the embargo. It may seem like the most obvious of dots to connect from our perspective, but even though there were glaring signs leading up to the crisis, oil price and supply was never the topic of concern before 1973 that it is today. Nowadays the balance of supply and demand is so delicate that it's important for you as a Forex trader to understand how currencies are correlated with oil prices (more on this later), as well as to keep abreast of any global events that could impact its supply. Finally, the oil crisis of 1973 also made energy conservation, a term largely absents from people's vocabularies at the time, a priority which has only grown more urgent as we move closer and closer to depleting our planet's fossil fuel reserves.

Cooperative Central Bank Intervention. The Plaza Accord of 1985.

You may have observed an interesting dynamic at work in the brief history of forex we have outlined so far; a certain pull and push between the need for overt regulation and control, versus a laissez-faire approach in which a free market can regulate itself. If you have identified this theme you are right to do so, the two opposing drives are always present, with proponents of the former most vocal in the wake of an economic crisis, and advocates for the latter seeming to have free rein when all is well in the global economy. The fears that led to Bretton Woods in the first place, and to Nixon wanting to keep exchange rates fixed in the Smithsonian Agreement, were precisely that if left to regulate itself competing devaluations between rival currencies and other antagonistic trade practices would lead to global instability.

Conversely, the short-comings of both Bretton Woods and the Smithsonian Agreement were made glaringly obvious by a market unwilling, or unable, to be locked down to the very same fixed relationships that were imposed to regulate it. And again, the period between the free-floating of the world's major currencies and the Plaza Accord would give lie to the myth that simple supply and demand dynamics are all that are required to regulate an efficient market.

We have already looked at the first major crisis to affect the global economy after the abandonment of Bretton Woods in 1971. The fourfold increase in the price of oil after the crisis of 1973 resulted in increased import expenditures for industrialised nations, upsetting their balance of payments. Recall that oil is priced in dollars, so the recycling of US dollars held by OPEC nations (petrodollar recycling) inevitably led to a h2 US dollar even though the United States continued to run a substantial trade deficit.

In the late 1970's the US dollar would fall in value as this growing deficit eroded investor confidence. This would be exacerbated by the Iranian revolution and the second oil shock of 1979, when OPEC again hiked the price of oil. However, by the early 1980s a hawkish stance from Federal Reserve chairman Paul Volcker, combined with renewed interest in the dollar as a safe haven currency after the outbreak of the Iran-Iraq war, helped dollar strength to return. 1980 would also be a watershed moment for oil as increased output from the USSR, Venezuela, Mexico, Nigeria, as well as the entry of Alaskan and North Sea oil, precipitated the start of a 20-year decline in oil prices, and a loosening of OPEC's grip.

Volcker's mandate to halt stagflation by raising US interest rates was successful, although an undesired consequence of his policies was that the dollar became overvalued. This resulted in US exports being expensive and uncompetitive (especially American cars), while imports became cheap, which put further pressure on US trade balance. Between 1980 and 1985 the US dollar appreciated by around 50% against the yen, the Deutsche mark, the sterling and the French franc.

The Plaza Accord, so called because it was signed at the Plaza hotel in New York, was an attempt to bring the economies of the United States, Japan, West Germany, the United Kingdom and France back into sync by devaluing the US dollar. When the agreement was made the US current account deficit had reached around 3.5% of the nation's GDP while its economy was growing by around 3%. Europe on the other hand had a large trade surplus and was experiencing negative growth of around -0.7%. To redress the balance, the G-5 agreed to a mixture of tax and public spending cuts, private sector expansion and the opening of markets.

Over the next couple of years, the US dollar would depreciate by 50% against the rest of the G-5 nations. By 1987 the Japanese yen had gone from 242 per dollar to 150 per dollar. The US trade deficit with Europe had also been successfully reduced, though not with Japan.

The US dollar would continue to drop beyond the agreed targets, prompting the then G-6 to negotiate the Louvre Accord, which was an effort to halt the US dollar's decline. This would prove to be a much trickier proposition than the devaluation of the Plaza accord. This is due to the dollar having already been during a downtrend at the time when the Plaza Accord was signed. On the other hand, the Louvre Accord would attempt to reverse an already well-established trend and do so through a sustained coordination of the economic policies of the 6 largest economies in the world. By 1988 the dollar was worth 121 yen and 1.57 Deutsche marks. A drastic increase in US interest rates was the only thing that would halt the downturn and strengthen the dollar.

The Plaza Accord was an important historical milestone in the development of the foreign exchange market. It was the first time that nations had agreed to actively intervene in a coordinated way so as to affect currency values, it was an example of how central bank interventions could be orchestrated across national borders in the interests of the global economy. It was also a moment in history when the broadest consequences of globalisation were there for all to see, and markets were shown to require an occasional guiding hand to be able to run smoothly and efficiently.

The Latin American Debt Crisis

In the 1980s much of Latin America was affected by a severe debt crisis which blighted the lives and stifled the opportunities of countless citizens, it would come to be known as La DécadaPerdida, or the lost decade.

So far, we have been sketching an outline of the global economy, tracking the way it has developed from the "beggar thy neighbour" policies leading up to the Great Depression, to today's global reality where a single surprise can have knock-on effects that are felt around the planet. We have seen how a valuable commodity in the hands of a few can be wielded like a weapon over the rest of the world, we've looked at the pull and push dynamic between regulation and free markets, and have observed how central banks can coordinate between themselves to affect exchange rates. One of the things you will observe as you immerse yourselves in the markets is that both leaving them to their own devices and attempting to control them inevitably lead to undesired outcomes.

One of the consequences of the oil crisis of the 1970s came about because of petrodollar recycling. The fact that oil is priced in US dollars led to OPEC nations accumulating a great deal of wealth when the price of oil was drastically increased. OPEC'spetro dollars inevitability found their way back into the banking system, partly due to many OPEC nations opting not to reinvest this capital into their own domestic infrastructures. The massive influx of petrodollar deposits significantly increased the lending capacity of the banks, and with the demand for loans among industrialised nations having fallen during the recession, a large amount of this money was loaned out to rapidly industrialising Latin American countries.

Latin America had been experiencing something of a boom in manufacturing from the 1930's onwards. Its newly industrialised economies had been focused on breaking their dependence on imported consumer goods from the developed world by building domestic industries to feed this demand. This process of import substitution industrialisation (ISI) had brought rapid growth to countries such as Mexico, Brazil and Argentina, but was nearing a ceiling in terms of possible future growth without renewed investment in the manufacture of heavier consumer goods such as cars.

During the oil crisis of 1973 soaring oil prices and a reduction in global production led to South American oil producers picking up the slack left by OPEC nations and exporting a great deal of oil to the United States. This situation was doomed to be short-lived though, and as the inflated prices settled after the crisis and production was ramped up again in the Middle East, economies such as Mexico's became economically unstable. Other South American net importers of oil suffered from increasing fuel bills during the crisis and higher debt repayments after the crisis as their western creditors raised interest rates.

The choice to carry on pursuing import substitution industrialisation rather than transitioning to export driven economies, was perhaps partially decided by the global economic climate of the time. The severe recession which had hit developed countries in the wake of the oil-shock meant that demand for imports had fallen drastically, as had the demand for raw materials, which also hurt South America's export market.

With interest rates rising in the west, especially in the United States where hawkish policies had been introduced by Fed chairman Paul Volker to ease stagflation (most of the commercial banks that had lent money to South America were US and Japanese), the cost of servicing these loans increased drastically. Rising interest rates had also helped restore confidence in the US dollar, which put pressure on Latin American exchange rates, further increasing both the value of their debts and the cost of their repayments. From 1975 to 1983 Latin America's debt had gone from $75 billion to $315 billion, the latter figure being around 50% of the region's GDP. The annual cost of servicing those loans had also risen from $12 billion in 1975 to $66 billion in 1982.

In August of 1982 it was announced by Mexico's Minister of finance, Jesus Silva-Herzog, that the country would not be able to continue servicing its existing loans. The loan market imploded overnight. Commercial banks stopped lending to the region and as most of the existing loans were short term in nature, the fact that banks were refusing to refinance them led to billions of dollars of debt being due all at once.

The resulting crisis would be the worst in the region's history. Unemployment shot up, incomes and spending power plummeted, growth ground to a halt and poverty increased as social programs were abandoned in favour of debt repayments. Between 1982 and 1985 Latin American economies contracted by around 9 percent. In order to refinance the existing loans countries were required to accept much stricter conditions as well as allowing the International Monetary Fund (IMF) to step in and introduce austerity measures and country-wide reforms, the most notable of which were the abandonment of import substitution industrialisation in favour of free market capitalism and the privatisation of industry.

The Asian Financial Crisis of 1997

The Asian financial crisis occurred in 1997-98 and revealed just how interconnected the global currency markets are. One of our on-going themes in this brief history of forex has been how central banks and governments have sought to intervene in the markets; the Asian crisis revealed once and for all how powerless these institutions can be when attempting to act against overwhelming market forces and unsustainable fundamentals.

Leading up to the crisis the economies of Southeast Asia had been particularly attractive for investors owing to their impressive growth rates. The four Asian Tigers (Hong Kong, Singapore, South Korea and Taiwan) had rapidly developed into formidable global economies specialising in finance and manufacturing, followed closely by what came to be known as the Tiger Cub economies of Malaysia, Indonesia, Thailand and Philippines. These economies in particular had been rapidly expanding and were attracting a great deal of speculative investment due to the high interest rates they maintained. Thailand was an economic miracle, experiencing growth of just below 10% per year for more than a decade preceding the crisis. It would also eventually prove to be the weak link that set the crash in motion.

The precise causes of the crisis are, of course, numerous and still provoke debate; however, a combination of hot money fuelling unsustainable asset bubbles, poor lending practices leading to non-performing loans, ballooning current account deficits, the devaluation of the yen and renminbi, and the U.S recovering from recession are all cited as contributing factors.

A massive influx of foreign investment had led to there being a great deal of capital available for development loans, many of which ended up in the hands of individuals with nepotistic ties to government and banking officials, rather than those most eligible and best able to pay them back. Thailand, South Korea and Indonesia were running pretty hefty current account deficits, Thailand's in particular represented around 8% of the country's GDP and stood at just under $15 billion before the crash. In the wake of the Plaza Accord the devaluation of the yen and renminbi and the subsequent strengthening of the U.S dollar made Asian exports far less competitive. This further exacerbated current account deficits in the region. Factor in the Federal Reserve's interest rate hikes which led to capital flight back into the US economy, and you have a convergence of circumstances that led to a massive loss of confidence resulting in the speculative attacks of May 14 and 15 1997, which caused the eventual devaluation of the Thai baht.

A lack of foreign exchange reserves rendered the Thai government incapable of supporting the baht in the face of these attacks, the currency was eventually allowed to float on July 2, 1997, and swiftly lost more than half of its value while the Thai stock market dropped by 75%.

Within several months of the Thai crash the Indonesian rupiah and stock market reached record lows, causing the country's GDP to contract by around 13.5% that year.

The South Korean won also lost more than half of its value against the dollar, the country's credit rating was downgraded twice and its motor industry was kept alive by a series of mergers and acquisitions.

These three economies were the worst affected by the crisis, and were the beneficiaries of a $40 billion International Monetary Fund (IMF) initiative to restore economic balance to the region. However the knock-on effects of the crisis were far-reaching and led to a general economic slowdown that was felt across the globe. Investors had become increasingly risk averse when it came to developing markets. The ensuing economic slowdown also caused the price of oil to drop and was a contributing factor in the Russian financial crisis of 1998.

In the decade following the Asian crisis many countries in the region took steps to be much less reliant on hot money as an economic stimulant. They also started to run current account surpluses and built up their foreign exchange reserves so as to be able to support their respective currencies in the event of future speculative attacks. As a direct result of these measures Asia was far better able to weather the global financial crisis of 2008. The table below reveals the extent of China's growing foreign exchange reserves from 2004 up until the present day.

If you enjoyed this book or found it useful I'd be very grateful if you'd post a short review on Amazon. Your support really does make a difference and I read all the reviews personally, so I can get your feedback and make this book even better.

Thanks again for your support!

Thank you

www.ingramcontent.com/pod-product-compliance
Lightning Source LLC
Chambersburg PA
CBHW082204220526
45470CB00010B/3044